DATE DUE

D1248517

Opting for self-management

Although the main emphasis in the shift towards self-managing schools has been orchestrated through the introduction of local management of schools in the Education Reform Act, this development has been given radical impetus by the opportunity for schools to 'opt out' of local authority control and become grant-maintained. Opting out remains one of the more controversial provisions of the Education Reform Act, and one which has attracted a great deal of attention. The number of schools achieving grant-maintained status is steadily growing, increasing the importance of this group of schools and enhancing the interest in them both nationally and internationally, as moves towards decentralisation occur in other countries, such as New Zealand, Australia and the United States.

Opting for Self-Management examines the early experiences of the first grant-maintained schools and considers the challenges that face the self-managing school in the 1990s. The book looks at the context of the change of status, what it means to be grant-maintained, and reviews the types of schools that have opted out so far and their reasons for doing so. A section of specially commissioned case studies written by headteachers offers accounts of how each school has coped with the move to grant-maintained status. The book provides a practical and realistic appraisal of grant-maintained schools and their move towards self management, exploring both the advantages and disadvantages of opting out of local authority control.

Brent Davies is Principal Lecturer in Education Management at Leeds Polytechnic. He is a Visiting Professor at the University of Southern California, where he lectures on self-managing schools. He has published and lectured widely on education management in the UK and USA.

Lesley Anderson is Deputy Director of the Grant-Maintained Schools Centre, prior to which she taught and held various posts of responsibility in comprehensive schools. She is Visiting Professor at the University of Southern California and a Visiting Fellow at Leeds Polytechnic.

Educational management series
Edited by Cyril Poster

Opting for self-management

The early experience of
grant-maintained schools

Brent Davies and Lesley Anderson

ROUTLEDGE

London and New York

First published 1992
by Routledge
11 New Fetter Lane, London EC4P 4EE

Simultaneously published in the USA and Canada
by Routledge
a division of Routledge, Chapman and Hall, Inc.
29 West 35th Street, New York, NY 10001

Typeset from the authors' wordprocessing disks by
NWL Editorial Services, Langport, Somerset

Printed and bound in Great Britain by
Biddles Ltd, Guildford and King's Lynn

British Library Cataloguing in Publication Data
A catalogue reference for this title is available from the British Library

ISBN 0–415–07347–2

Library of Congress Cataloging in Publication Data
Davies, Brent, 1949–
Opting for self-management: the early experience of grant-
maintained schools / Brent Davies and Lesley Anderson.
p. cm. – (Educational management series)
Includes bibliographical references (p.) and index.
ISBN 0–415–07347–2
1. School management and organization – Great Britain.
I. Anderson, Lesley, 1951– . II. Title. III. Series.
LB2900.5.D38 1991   91–44378
371.2′00941–dc20   CIP

Contents

Part IV   Appendices

Preface

The introduction of grant-maintained status in the 1988 Education Reform Act and the subsequent opting out of Local Education Authority (LEA) control by schools has been one of the most controversial developments of the 1980s and early 1990s. This book does not set out to support or decry the move toward grant-maintained status. Instead it seeks to provide a commentary on this radical policy initiative in the education system and to document the experiences of the first schools to achieve such status. Documenting experience to date is very difficult because of the, as yet, limited life of most grant-maintained schools. However some commentary and documentation of experience is possible.

The book seeks to provide that commentary and documentation. To achieve this the book is split into four parts. The initial part provides two contextual information chapters. The first considers the moves towards decentralised management in a wider context and specifically examines the rationale for the change, the elements making up the change and the arguments for decentralisation. Having established this overview, the second chapter provides the factual information about the process of opting out and the nature and dimensions of a grant-maintained school.

With this initial understanding established, Part II draws on the experiences to date of representatives from the early schools to opt out. In a conference report in 1988 and a subsequent article Brent Davies coined the phrase 'no school with a flat roof can ever opt out!' Experience has shown this not to be the case and the reasons for opting out are many and various. While threat of closure or reorganisation proved to be early motivators, the desire for self-management is increasingly the dominant reason. Why and how schools opt out and how they organise the key elements of school management form the basis of Part II with five headteachers and one chairman of governors each taking an issue in managing a grant-maintained school.

In Chapter 3 Cecil Knight provides (through a case study of his school) a stimulating account of the process of opting out. This involved considerable controversy and legal challenge before grant-maintained status was achieved. Chapter 4 provides an account by Roger Perks of how he is developing a management approach to establish a grant-maintained ethos in his school to maximise the advantage of this change of status. How schools manage their new financial responsibilities is discussed by Keith Barker in Chapter 5 and the complexities of managing capital development and contracts is covered in Chapter 6 by Brother Francis. The potentially controversial distinction between governing and managing and the role of governors in self- managing schools is tackled by Ray Page in Chapter 7. Finally, in the last chapter in this part, Jennifer Morris describes how she manages staff development in the framework of a grant-maintained school.

To provide perspectives to stimulate the debate on grant-maintained schools, Part III discusses the advantages (Chapter 9) and disadvantages (Chapter 10) of grant-maintained status. These chapters are followed by a final one which looks at the management thinking that is necessary to run an effective self-managing school in the 1990s.

Part IV provides, in Appendix form, data on grant-maintained schools to set in context much of the information that is presented in this book.

The number of schools achieving grant-maintained status is steadily growing; the rate of increase is subject to national political debate. (The authors completed this book in September 1991 at a time when a general election was pending!) This book has not sought to engage in political advocacy but to provide a stimulus for discussion. We hope the reader will find it provides that stimulus.

REFERENCE

Davies B. (1988) 'No school with a flat roof can ever opt out', *Organisational Change and Development*, 9 (2).

ACKNOWLEDGEMENTS

The authors would like to acknowledge the Assistant Masters and Mistresses Association (AMMA) for their permission to publish significant parts of their questionnaire survey results (June 1991) and Michael Pavey of the Company of Designers for advice and guidance on capital development.

Part I

Chapter 1

The context and the rationale for grant-maintained status

This chapter aims to outline the forces that have heralded the move towards opting out and grant-maintained status. It considers:

- the context of change to grant-maintained status;
- the rationale for the change;
- the nature of the change;
- the arguments for the change.

By establishing this broad review and perspective it will enable the reader to set in context the rest of the book which examines practice to date.

THE CONTEXT OF THE CHANGE

The revolution in the English education system that the 1988 Education Reform Act (ERA) engineered will have far-reaching consequences for our schools in the 1990s. One of the significant elements in these reforms has been the establishment of grant-maintained schools. While this book obviously focuses on grant-maintained schools, it would be a mistake to view this development in isolation from the overall changes that are occurring in education, both nationally and internationally. In both these contexts there have been considerable movements towards decentralisation and self-managing institutions.

On a national basis, the move in April 1989 of polytechnics and colleges of higher education away from LEA control to incorporated bodies was a clear example of central government's intention to create self-managing institutions in the higher education sector. At school level, the move towards Local Management of Schools (LMS), as presented in the 1988 ERA, heralds the most significant change in the running of schools since the 1944 Education Act. Subsequent changes since the ERA have meant that all LEAs will have to delegate 85 per cent of the potential schools budget to the school level and, of that schools budget, 80 per cent must be directly linked by a formula to the number of pupils. However, far more radical than this move towards self-managing LEA schools has been the legislation to make schools independent of their LEAs by allowing them to opt out of local control by seeking grant-maintained status and thereafter receive funding directly from the Department of Education and Science (DES). The development of City Technology Colleges (CTCs) also mirrors this move towards self-managing institutions that are outside the control of local education authorities. Additionally, the more recent plans to restructure 16–19 education by taking away from LEAs control of sixth form colleges and colleges of further education are yet other examples of continuing moves towards decentralisation of management control in this sector.

Internationally, similar moves towards decentralisation have been seen in Australia and, more radically, in New Zealand with the abolition of LEAs and the establishment of local school management. On the continent further examples of greater school-based independence are found in the Netherlands and Belgium. A good overview of this is provided by Hill, Oakley Smith and Spinks (1990). The situation is much more complex in the USA. The separation of powers between the federal government and individual states means that national reorganisation is impossible. Early attempts at greater school-based reforms in several states have had varying degrees of success. Influenced by the reforms in Edmonton, Canada, the 1990s are seeing a second wave of the decentralisation movement in the USA. Here the significant factors are the way in which decentralisation has been linked to the pressures on the education system for reform and restructuring to improve the quality of teaching and learning. Notable examples are provided by Kentucky, Florida and particularly by California, where the Los Angeles Unified School District reflects a bottom-up, teacher-led movement for reform which entails teachers gaining control of resources in order to improve the standard of education offered in the schools.

While these national and international changes reflect pressure to increase both educational and financial decision-making at the school level, nothing is so radical as the grant-maintained movement in the UK. Most significantly, grant-maintained schools do not merely represent a function or part of the decentralisation movement, but are symbolic of a much more radical change in the relationship between central government, LEAs and schools. They are indeed at the forefront of the restructuring movement which creates a new relationship between central government and local schools at the expense of the traditional relationship and partnership between local and central government. As a result of the changes in the 1988 ERA, central government has increased its control significantly over various areas of schooling, the best example being the control of the curriculum through the establishment of a National Curriculum. At the same time central government has significantly reduced the power and scope of LEAs to determine and control education and schools locally. What is emerging is a polarisation of the education system, with more power at the centre and at the school level, and little or none at LEA level. Grant-maintained schools can be seen as the fundamental example of this polarisation of the system in their establishment as self-managing institutions with central funding.

THE RATIONALE FOR THE CHANGE

Concern about the output of the education system has grown from a variety of sources in the UK. This can be traced back over a number of years, but perhaps the most significant turning point was the Great Debate initiated by the then Prime Minister, James Callaghan, in 1976, when he responded to the widespread concern about standards in education. Various pressure groups were also producing documents, such as the famous 'Black Papers' which purported to show a decline in standards. This background influenced government policy during the 1980s and culminated in the 1988 ERA. This is best seen as being based on the need both to reform and to restructure education; mere adjustments to the existing system were not considered enough by themselves to bring about the desired improvement in the quality of education delivered in our schools.

Concern about school performance existed in terms of:

- underachievement of pupils;
- the lack of a basic curriculum for all pupils;
- the lack of standard tests for children at different ages so that parents could monitor their children's progress.

These concerns have been addressed to a large degree by reforms such as the establishment of a National Curriculum and the development of national testing for pupils at four key age stages. However, there is also a view that these reforms in themselves would not produce an improvement in educational standards without the driving force of a restructured school system. This is based on a number of criticisms of the present system:

- that there is a lack of accountability by schools to their clients. There had been 'producer-capture' in that those providing or producing education, the teachers, were too dominant in determining policy and access and not fully accountable for their activities.
- that there was a lack of choice in the system. It was felt that parents should be given far greater choice over the school that their children might attend.
- that LEAs were overly bureaucratic and politically motivated and did not allow schools the freedom to manage their own affairs.
- that schools were not managing resources to achieve the best results for their pupils because resource allocation decisions were taken elsewhere. There was no competition or incentive to schools to develop and provide specialist provision for their particular locality.

Given these criticisms of the system, a method of liberating the creative energies of schools to provide more effective education for their pupils was perceived as a necessity for the 1990s. The way to achieve this was structured into a system that provided the individual schools with control within a market framework. The advent of grant-maintained schools is therefore perceived by its supporters as a method of providing the creative structural framework in which to drive through the educational reforms necessary for an improved education system.

THE NATURE OF THE CHANGE

This change is a radical shift which moves from the perspective of corporate and comprehensive provision to one where strength through diversity is perceived as a method of improving the school system. It can be seen as a move from a social democratic framework to a consumer democratic framework. A social democratic framework implies that institutional organisation is part of a comprehensive state provision with management in the hands of regionally elected bodies, whereas a consumer democracy sees institution management as the basis of school organisation. When it comes to the exercise of government power, this shift represents a move from centralised planning, based on a partnership between central and local government with electoral accountability, to one which emphasises market competition and consumer choice with a link between the centre and the consumer which stresses public choice and accountability.

This change in the structure of the school system puts grant-maintained schools in the forefront of the market environment. The dynamic nature of this process can be illustrated by considering some of the following key factors that form this new competitive market environment:

- financial delegation;
- formula funding;
- open enrolment;
- performance indicators;
- site-based management.

Financial delegation

This involves the school having complete control of its finance. Having received its funding from the DES in the form of an annual maintenance grant (AMG), it is free to allocate this income over the range of expenditure headings in the school budget. Chapter 5 provides an account of this process. The significant difference between grant-maintained and LMS schools is that, in the former, the amount previously retained by the LEA for property maintenance, central administration, advisory and inspection services, legal and accounting services and other support services is now given direct to the school. At the time of writing this is calculated as 16 per cent on top of the amount the school would have received if it had remained an LMS school. The school has, in effect, to run as a small business, to set up its own financial system and be responsible for handling the money and spending it in an appropriate way to meet its educational objectives.

This last point is the key element in delegated school management in grant-maintained schools. Whereas establishing a new school-based financial control system is important for the smooth running of the school, the critical factors are the management process and decisions that determine the allocation of funds to alternative expenditure headings. The choice of the number and type of teaching and support staff, their relative salaries and allowances in balance with the need for learning materials, and the demands of maintaining the premises provides the key budgetary decision area. The moves towards a resource management framework rather than a mere bookkeeping system is one of the significant challenges that headteachers and senior staff face in this new environment.

Previously, prior to LMS, schools will have received staffing and other resource allocations in centrally determined numbers and amounts. Self-management provides the flexibility and freedom for each school to determine its individual resource needs. Staffing presents a good example of this change. Where previously a fixed number of staff would have been provided according to the standard pupil–teacher ratio, now the number of staff in the school is determined by the total budget and the relative price of teachers according to their point on the salary scale and any responsibility allowance allocated to them. Making these resource choices in the staffing area and in competition with other expenditure demands is a new skill that managers have to exercise under the grant-maintained and LMS framework.

Probably the most significant element in this is attempting to relate different combinations of expenditure to learning output achieved by pupils. The rationale of delegated school management, and grant-maintained status in particular, is that the new-found management freedom and responsibility is not an end in itself, but that it should improve not only the learning and teaching process but also the learning outcomes of pupils.

This, however, does present two problems for schools. Their experience to date of relating expenditure decisions to output is minimal and indeed the whole process is very complex anyway. Second, the financial and educational decision-making processes in LEA schools have traditionally been incremental and to move to a zero-based approach where all resource devices are reassessed to see if they meet the organisational objectives is not easy as a way of thinking or as a way of allocating resources.

The challenge remains, however, to ensure that the financial delegation which gives resource decision-making power to grant-maintained schools does not end up merely as an abstract managerial activity. It should be that it enables the school more fully to meet its learning and teaching objectives. The long-term evaluation of the first cohorts of schools which opted out will not be whether grant-maintained status enabled them to preserve the existing *status quo* in terms of present structures, like keeping grammar school status or even preventing closure, but how they have used the financial freedom of delegated finance to change existing patterns not only to maintain but to enhance and improve learning outcomes.

Formula funding

Schools have traditionally been funded on an historical cost basis which had been adjusted annually as part of an incrementally-based budgetary cycle. The introduction of LMS has made the funding of LEA schools dependent on formula funding based on pupil numbers for at least 80 per cent of their budget, with the remaining amount determined by other factors such as premises and protection for small schools. In grant-maintained schools the calculation of their annual maintenance grant is based on the same LEA LMS formula as it would have been had they remained within the local authority plus an additional 16 per cent to account for central LEA costs which are now passed on to the school. Thus the formula is driven largely by pupil numbers as in LMS schools and, when combined with open enrolment, produces a considerable market accountability on the schools as more pupils means more funding and vice versa.

Open enrolment

With the vast majority of the funding for grant-maintained schools determined by pupil numbers under the formula funding mechanism, the open enrolment policy of the government has a dramatic effect. Parents are free to choose the school to which to send their children, and, as children move around the system, the funding follows them. This is, in effect, a voucher system within the state education sector. Therefore, decisions by parents and children about which school to choose have a direct and immediate effect on each individual school's budget. As children move around the system, schools that gain pupils also gain resources and the ability to buy more teachers and more equipment. Conversely, schools that lose pupils are in exactly the opposite position. Open enrolment, when linked to formula funding, provides a dimension of market accountability to sit beside the school's traditional dimension of educational accountability. This makes parental choice the key factor in determining the success and viability of a school.

Performance indicators

In judging and assessing schools, the use of performance indicators is becoming more widespread. Schools are basing their attempt at formulating performance indicators on the *aide-memoire* on 'School Indicators for Internal Management' (DES, 1988). This lists six main criteria:

- basic school data;
- school context;
- pupil achievement;
- parental involvement;
- pupil attitudes;
- management.

However, whereas schools often concentrate on these overt performance indicators using measures such as examination pass rates or other ability assessments, parents use both these and other factors. A second set of performance indicators which could be considered as covert is also critical in forming client opinion. These are not directly educational but are nevertheless very influential. Examples include the wearing of school uniform or the behaviour of the pupils on the school buses. Schools therefore have to address both overt and covert performance indicators.

Site-based management

Site-based mangement brings together these four factors in a new, dynamic relationship. The significance for grant-maintained schools is how they interrelate. How parents perceive a school will affect their decision about the one they choose for their children. These decisions, made collectively by parents, will determine the amount of the financially delegated budget that the school receives through the formula funding mechanism. In this market environment, it is not sufficient to believe that 'virtue brings its own reward' as, to succeed, schools have not only to provide good education but also to be perceived as doing so. This therefore leads us to rewrite the statement thus: 'While virtue may not bring its own reward, virtue with a good marketing strategy, may.'

The task for school site-based managers is to define roles, responsibilities and participation by the partners – the governors, the headteacher, the staff, parents and pupils – in managing the school to meet the challenge of this new environment. It is, as always, the effective management of the teaching and learning process that is critical. However the factors – financial delegation, formula funding, open enrolment, performance indicators and site-based management – give schools the powers to achieve this in a market environment and drive them to be more responsive to their clients. The significance is that success or failure, survival or closure depends on how the partners at the school level make the decisions to best provide the education for their children.

THE ARGUMENTS FOR THE CHANGE

While individual headteachers and one chairman of governors of six grant-maintained schools will describe in detail the benefits of opting out and becoming responsible for self-managing schools, it is worth reflecting generally on the advantages of self-management. These can be considered in three main areas:

- flexibility;
- productivity;
- accountability.

Flexibility

The main argument for grant-maintained status centres on the fact that, given the freedom from bureaucratic LEA control, schools can respond more effectively to their clients' needs. They will be able to determine precisely the mix of resources in terms of teachers, support staff, materials, equipment and premises that meet the needs of pupils as determined by the school itself. They will also be able to respond quickly to changes in these needs and demands.

The freedom to do this is certainly established through grant-maintained status. However, the ability to make resource choices and to understand how different choices affect learning outcomes is not one that schools have had control over and thus practised for very long. Whether they use this new-found flexibility to rethink the teaching/learning process in a creative way or whether they follow past incremental patterns will determine a great deal of the success of grant-maintained schools in this most important area.

Productivity

It follows that this greater flexibility offers considerable opportunity to increase the productivity of the schools. Productivity in this context refers to the quality and quantity of education that children receive. By more closely relating resource decisions to clients' needs, increased efficiency is achieved through maximising resource use and educational outputs. The only significant evaluation of grant-maintained schools is whether the children attending them receive a better education than they would elsewhere or would have done previously in that school. Flexibility in itself is useless; it is only valuable if it achieves this increase in learning outcomes. The task facing grant-maintained schools is to move away from the organisational and managerial focus of the transition from LEA-control to grant-maintained status and to concentrate on these learning outcomes.

Accountability

Grant-maintained schools in this new framework should be more accountable to their clients for the quality of the education they provide. There are two mechanisms for this. First, it is made possible through the reformed structure and enhanced powers of the governing body. This enables much more effective and immediate control of the school by its local community. Second, the market mechanism will ensure that schools that are popular with parents are rewarded by formula funding and hence resources, with the opposite being true of unsuccessful schools. How this empowers teachers in the classroom to be more accountable and responsible for the quality of education they deliver is an important dimension of real accountability in the school. This also provides a major challenge for grant-maintained schools.

CONCLUSION

This chapter sets the concept of grant-maintained schools in the context of the wider movement to delegated site-based management. The critical factor in evaluating this policy development is provided by the final section which argues that if grant-maintained status provides a benefit it should be in terms of improved flexibility, productivity and accountability of the schools. The next chapter provides the necessary detailed information to understand the technical nature of grant-maintained schools and the opting out process.

REFERENCES

DES (1988) *Aide-Memoire on School Indicators for Internal Management*, London: DES.
Hill D., Oakley Smith B. and Spinks J. (1990) *Local Management of Schools*, London: Paul Chapman Publishing.

Chapter 2

How schools achieve grant-maintained status

This chapter provides a factual account of the nature and dimensions of grant-maintained status. It is included to enable the reader to have a clear, conceptual understanding of what it means for a school to be grant-maintained. It considers the nature of grant-maintained schools, which schools can apply for the status, how the schools are funded, what it means for staff to work in a grant-maintained school and how a school becomes grant-maintained.

WHAT IS A GRANT-MAINTAINED SCHOOL?

Compulsory and free education has been the right of all young people in Great Britain for over a hundred years. In order to deliver this service, different governments have set up various types of school within the state-maintained sector. Despite their differences, in terms of their intake and the curriculum offered, they have all been controlled and funded in the same way through local government, via an LEA.

Grant-maintained schools are a new category of state school created as part of the 1988 Education Reform Act and offer free education for all their pupils. They differ from LEA-controlled schools in so far as the governors of a grant-maintained school have total responsibility for every aspect of the running and functioning of the school. To achieve this, the governors receive public funding directly from the Secretary of State for Education and Science. It is important to emphasise that a grant-maintained school is not a private or independent school: on achieving the status it continues to offer free education.

WHICH SCHOOLS CAN APPLY TO BECOME GRANT-MAINTAINED?

Primary, middle or secondary LEA-controlled schools, but not nursery or special schools, can, after satisfying certain criteria, apply to the Secretary of

State to become grant-maintained. The final decision on whether an applicant school becomes grant-maintained rests with the Secretary of State.

The grant-maintained sector includes every type of school from the above categories: large city comprehensive schools as well as small rural primary schools, middle schools, schools with sixth forms, single sex and co-educational schools. Some of them offer selective education and others have religious foundations.

Until recently the governors of a grant-maintained school were not entitled to change the character of the school, that is the intake in terms of age-range, ability, gender or religious denomination, for at least five years after achieving the status, and then only after making application to the Secretary of State. However, this time restriction was removed in April 1991 and the governors are now free to apply for a change of character at any time if they so wish.

Grant-maintained schools do have many areas of commonality with LEA schools. They are all obliged to teach the National Curriculum and to assess and report on their pupils' progress according to national criteria and guidelines. Similarly, the teachers are required to take part in an appraisal scheme based upon the same criteria as those used in LEA schools.

HOW A SCHOOL BECOMES GRANT-MAINTAINED

Prior to making an application to become grant-maintained, it is necessary for there to be a ballot of the parents of the pupils registered at the school. This ballot can be triggered in one of two ways: either a resolution to this effect is passed at a meeting of the governing body and confirmed by a second resolution at a further meeting held not less than twenty-eight days and not more than forty-two days later; or a petition is given or sent to the chair or clerk of the governing body from the parents at the school. It is necessary for this petition to be supported by the parents of at least 20 per cent of the pupils registered at the school.

As soon as a ballot is requested or required, the governors are obliged to contact the Electoral Reform Society (ERS) without delay and to hold a ballot. The ERS has authority from the Secretary of State to claim from the DES the costs it incurs as a result of its work with the schools.

The ballot

The ballot is only valid if conducted by the ERS. The governors are responsible for providing the society with the electoral roll, details of the proposed initial governing body should the application prove successful, and the date on which it is proposed that the school would open with its new status. The governors must make available to staff in the school all the information which the Act requires parents to receive in connection with the ballot and must consider whether to supply the information to parents in languages other than English.

For these purposes the electoral roll comprises the name and address of every person recorded in the school's admissions register as being a parent of a registered pupil at the school. The initiative lies with the person wanting to be recorded on the admissions register as the parent of a particular child to ensure that his or her name is included on the register. Each parent, regardless of the number of children in a family who attend the school, has one vote.

The ERS sends each voter the necessary factual information and a ballot paper to be returned in a pre-paid envelope by a given date. The ERS is responsible for counting the votes and for sending the certified result to the governing body and the DES. If a simple majority of those who ballot are in favour of applying for grant-maintained status, and 50 per cent or more of those eligible to vote have done so, then the governors can go ahead and prepare a formal application to the Secretary of State.

However, if fewer than 50 per cent of those eligible to vote have done so, the ballot is disregarded, whatever the result. In these circumstances a second ballot must be held within fourteen days of the announcement of the result of the first. The second ballot is decisive, irrespective of the turnout. In cases where the ballot goes against making application for the status, it is not normal for the governing body to pass a second resolution or receive a petition from parents to hold another ballot until more than twelve months from the date of the preceding ballot result. However, in cases where the school's circumstances have changed markedly, the Secretary of State may consider such a request.

The proposals for grant-maintained status

The governors of a school where the ballot is in favour of seeking grant-maintained status are required to prepare and publish their proposal within six months of the result of the ballot. The proposal is required to provide information for the Secretary of State to help him reach his decision and to inform members of the public who may wish to comment.

The proposal sets out details about the school and how it will be managed. These include:

- the names and addresses of governors and the categories within which they are nominated, elected or co-opted;
- the proposed date of incorporation to grant-maintained status;
- arrangements for the admission of pupils;
- arrangements for the provision for pupils with special educational needs;
- arrangements for the induction and in-service training of teachers.

In addition, the proposal must include factual information about the school – its character, its category and the number of pupils for whom accommodation can be provided – as well as details of the ballot result.

Once the proposal is complete the governors are required to publish it, observing certain rules. The proposal must be available for inspection both at the school and at some other local public building. As soon as the two-month period for objections has expired the Secretary of State decides whether the school will become grant-maintained based upon his view of the merits in the proposal and any comments which have been put to him. He may approve or reject the proposal, or after consulting the proposers he may approve subject to some modification to, for example, the date of incorporation. He also has the option of requiring the governing body to do further work on a proposal which he has rejected and to publish the revised proposal within some given time-scale.

The transition to grant-maintained status

After the Secretary of State approves a school for grant-maintained status the school enters the transitional period, a time for the proposed initial governing body to prepare for the transfer of responsibilities which takes place on the date agreed by the Secretary of State. During the transitional period, the governing body may only exercise certain powers which the Secretary of State confers on them in order to prepare for incorporation. The powers include rights such as appointing non-teaching staff to carry out work in connection with the transfer, appointing teaching staff to take up appointment after incorporation, entering into contracts for the supply of goods and services which are required for the purpose or in connection with the functioning of the school after incorporation, and repudiating other contracts. They also have the right to hold meetings on the school premises. Additionally, the governors of a grant-maintained school in its transitional period may apply to the Secretary of State for further powers if they think it is necessary and appropriate. Most commonly governors apply for additional transitional powers relating to their school's admissions policy.

HOW A GRANT-MAINTAINED SCHOOL IS FUNDED

The governors of a grant-maintained school receive income in the form of grants paid directly to them by the DES. These include a one-off set-up grant, formula funded grants and grants for which schools must submit bids.

The transitional grant

The first allocation of funding the governors receive is a one-off transitional grant made available to them after the school has been approved for the status, but not yet incorporated. Secondary schools and large primary schools receive £30,000 plus £30 per pupil up to a maximum of £60,000. Primary schools with fewer than 200 pupils are paid a transitional grant at the rate of £20,000 plus £30 per pupil.

This grant may be used by the governors to cover expenditure incurred as part of the preparation for grant-maintained status. The governors are required to apply in writing to the DES giving details of their preparation plans and the necessary expenses. The types of expenditure envisaged for this grant can be classified as follows:

- Computer equipment including both hardware and software required for administrative purposes.
- Payroll including the purchasing of a system and necessary training or setting up a contract with a bureau.
- Office accommodation and costs including adaption of existing accommodation for increased staffing, the purchasing of additional office equipment and stationery resulting from the period of preparation.
- Administration including additional services that may be required at this time. Governors may decide to appoint and commence the employment of an administrator/bursar during this period.
- Appointments including the potential necessity to advertise, pay travel, subsistence and other incidental expenses in relation to recruiting and appointing staff. Addi tionally, governors may decide to appoint or, more likely, extend the role of members of staff already on the payroll to co-ordinate and oversee the preparations for grant-maintained status in order that they can focus on the strategic planning.
- Professional fees where it may be necessary to seek professional advice from solicitors, accountants or consultants.
- Governor training that may be required during the transitional period.
- Governor and staff expenses that may result from attendance at meetings or seminars in connection with the status.

Although the transitional grant is intended for expenditure incurred during the period prior to incorporation, it is possible that the transition to grant-maintained status extends beyond this date: for example, where accommodation is being adapted for new administrative staff. In these circumstances it is possible for part of this grant to be spent after incorporation.

The annual maintenance grant (AMG)

This is the governors' main source of revenue funding and is used to meet the normal running costs of the school. It is based upon the LMS formula of the school's former LEA and is paid to them on incorporation and thereafter in monthly instalments. For a school incorporated on or after 1 April 1991 the AMG is calculated as follows: LMS funding (including any safety net or phased introduction) as paid by the LEA, plus 16 per cent of the school's direct (LMS) AMG level, plus school meals and milk – an extra allocation based on a formula. For schools operating as grant-maintained schools before 1 April 1990 the amount paid in 1991–92 is either 16 per cent or the full-year cash amount as previously calculated by the DES as the school's share of LEA central spending in 1990–91 if this is higher.

The calculation above can be applied to any school as long as the LEA that it formerly belonged to has an approved LMS formula. For schools where this does not exist, the DES calculates this share of the central funding by basing it on the historical funding if it is a new grant-maintained school, or, if it is an established grant-maintained school, on the AMG calculated for the first full or part year of the status. The amount of the grant is reclaimed by the Secretary of State from the school's former LEA.

The AMG expenditure is monitored by the DES by requiring the schools to make monthly, quarterly and annual returns to them and by means of an annual audit.

Special purpose grants (SPG)

These may be made available for particular purposes in order to ensure a similar approach to grant-maintained schools to LEA schools. They may be paid as a one-off grant or on an indefinite basis and, to date, have been used for the following purposes:

- SPG(D) development: to parallel the GEST funding available to LEA schools for the in-service training of staff, the training of governors and curriculum development.
- SPG(R) restructuring: to provide assistance with the costs of compensation payments arising from approved restructuring of the teaching force provided that it is initiated during the first year after incorporation.
- SPG(P) premises: to assist schools meet the costs of insuring their premises; 50 per cent of the premium is paid up to a ceiling figure of £6,000.
- SPG(V) VAT: to compensate for additional VAT liabilities.

Capital grants

A capital allocation may be made available to the sector as a whole and, to date, has been presented in two parts. First, a formula funded allowance is paid each year to each school. This grant must be used for expenditure of a capital nature and cannot be used for maintenance, redecoration or day-to-day repairs. The governors are required to submit to the DES proposed expenditure plans together with estimated costs. The grant is for one year only and there are no carry-over facilities. In 1991–92 it was paid at the rate of £19,500 plus £9 per pupil.

Second, a global sum is allocated by the Secretary of State each year on the basis of bids received from the schools. In making their bids the governors are required to describe their plans for named capital projects costing more than £6,000.

Each bid is considered on its own merits, priority being given to schools with the most pressing needs. These include on-going projects to which schools were committed by their former maintaining authority, health and safety issues, and capital development required for the introduction of the National Curriculum. The level of the grant is 100 per cent.

Other grants

Other grants, such as Section 11 (extra teaching support for pupils whose first language is not English) and TVEI (Technical and Vocational Educational Initiative) are paid as appropriate to the school.

Many of the above grants have already, at the time of writing, been subject to change and there are no guarantees that they will not alter again or even be withdrawn.

THE ROLE OF A GRANT-MAINTAINED SCHOOL'S GOVERNING BODY

The governing body of a grant-maintained school is equivalent to the executive board in a commercial business. It has corporate status and can be sued. The governors are the employers and have responsibility not only for the school budget but also for ensuring that the activities and action taken in the name of the school are appropriate and within the law.

The instrument and articles of government for each grant-maintained school are made by the Secretary of State after consultation with the governors. These documents set out the constitution and functions of the governors and the headteacher, and the procedures which they have to adopt in particular circumstances.

The duties and responsibilities of the governors of a grant-maintained school are similar to those of the governors of an LEA-maintained school and derive in the main from the ERA. For example, the school has to provide a broad and balanced curriculum which, for pupils of compulsory school age, incorporates the National Curriculum, and must make provision for daily collective worship and religious education. In addition the school is subject to inspection by HMI, must account for the way in which it spends public money and must observe regulations relating to the employment of teachers and other staff. For a more detailed description of the duties and responsibilities of the governors of a grant-maintained school, the reader is referred to Leonard (1988).

The governors of a school approved for grant-maintained status have certain transitional powers from the date of the letter of approval. These are mainly linked to the ways in which they may use the transitional grant, the details of which were given in the previous section. Additionally, these powers entitle the governors to hold meetings on the school premises. The DES can, and does, grant additional transitional powers to a governing body of an approved grant-maintained school where it is felt necessary to ensure that the school will be prepared for incorporation.

The governing body of a grant-maintained school is made up from parents of pupils attending the school, teachers working at the school and people from the local community. At schools which have a foundation or trust, that is, those schools which were formerly voluntary-aided or controlled (religious denomination schools), the community representation is provided by the foundation governors. At former county schools, it is provided by *first* governors; the word 'first' describing their predominance on the governing body. These first governors form a new category within the governing body and are appointed by the other governors. This model of the appointment of governors is based upon the approach used in the voluntary-aided sector and is adopted to provide maximum continuity. The reader is referred once again to Leonard (1988) for further details.

The membership of grant-maintained school governing bodies is made up as follows:

- five parent governors, elected by the parents of pupils at the school;
- at least one but not more than two teacher governors, elected by the teachers at the school;
- the headteacher;
- a number of first or foundation governors greater than the total number of other governors.

Elected teacher and parent governors serve for four years; the first or foundation governors are expected to provide an element of greater continuity. The governing body decides their length of service which must be between five and seven years.

WHAT GRANT-MAINTAINED STATUS MEANS FOR STAFF

Although at the time of the ballot the staff of a school seeking grant-maintained status have no precise role in the process, the governors are required to make available to them the information parents receive. This includes the names and addresses of governors and the categories within which they were nominated, elected or co-opted. If the ballot is successful, then the staff of the school must have an opportunity to see the proposals and they can send objections to the Secretary of State. The elected teacher governors and the headteacher, if a member of the governing body, do of course retain their democratic rights and have the opportunity to be involved fully in the discussions in the governing body meetings.

At the time of incorporation

Staff, both teaching and non-teaching, already employed exclusively at the school when it becomes grant-maintained have the right to remain in employment at the school and there are few differences in the basic requirements of their work or in their rights. The governing body, not the LEA, now becomes their employer and most of the former responsibilities of the LEA in connection with their employment are directly transferred. Contracts of employment automatically transfer from the LEA to the school on the day it begins its new status.

The exceptions to this apply to staff who are not employed exclusively at the school or who are providing meals as part of a service for the school in question and at the same time for other schools or institutions within the LEA. However, it is possible for special arrangements to be made for such staff to transfer to the employment of the school. Additionally, there may be staff working at the school who are not employed by the LEA or by the governing body, for example, contract cleaning staff. In these circumstances the contracts of the employees obviously remain with the third party. However, when the contracted service is retained by the governing body it may well be possible for such staff to continue to work at the school.

Staff rights and conditions of service

The staff in a grant-maintained school are protected in their employment by the standard employment legislation and other relevant employment-related legislation, such as the Race Relations and Sex Discrimination Acts and the Health and Safety at Work Act. The Instrument and Articles of Government of a grant-maintained school require the governing body to establish and set down their own grievance and disciplinary procedures. As with other employment, staff have the right to take the governing body to an industrial tribunal if they believe they have been unfairly dismissed.

When staff move between a grant-maintained and an LEA school, their reckonable service for pension purposes and redundancy entitlement is not broken when they take up the new appointment. Entitlement to other, non-statutory benefits may be negotiated between the employer and the employee. Similarly, when a governing body decides it is in the interests of the school, a member of staff may be offered early retirement. The regulations for this are the same as those applying in an LEA school and include the possibility for the governing body to pay an enhancement of up to ten years.

A significant implication of self-management, be it grant-maintained status or LMS, is the opportunity for governors to decide how many staff they will employ and at what level of salary. The governors are free to spend the money at their disposal on staff or other resources, taking account of the advice of the senior staff about the needs of the school in respect of the delivery of an effective education and their requirement to provide those items previously supplied by the LEA.

Until recently teachers' pay arrangements in grant-maintained schools were necessarily governed by the national arrangements set out in the current School Teachers' Pay and Conditions document. However, from 1992, individual grant-maintained schools, as well as individual LEA schools, are able to opt out of the national arrangements and the governors may themselves settle the pay and conditions of their own teachers.

Staff roles, responsibilities and development

As stated previously, the role of a teacher working in a grant-maintained school is the same as in an LEA school. They are required to teach the National Curriculum and be involved in the appropriate assessment and testing. They are required to report to parents in the same way as in an LEA school and to follow statutory guidelines on such issues as National Records of Achievement and schoolteacher appraisal.

The governors of grant-maintained schools are required to make suitable arrangements for the induction and support of newly-qualified teachers and the statutory regulations on probation apply equally to grant-maintained schools, except that the probation decisions are made by the governing body and not the LEA. A teacher who has successfully completed probation in a grant-maintained school is not required to repeat it on appointment to an LEA school.

With regard to the in-service training of teachers, the governors of a grant-maintained school are required to set out in the proposal for grant-maintained status their intentions for the professional development of their staff. They receive a special purpose grant for such training in addition to being able to draw on their general funds.

CONCLUSION

This chapter has provided the detailed factual information on what a grant-maintained school is, the way a school achieves the status and some of the implications for those associated with this type of school. It concludes Part I of the book and is now followed by accounts in Part II of the practical experiences from six grant-maintained schools.

REFERENCE

Leonard M. (1988) *The 1988 Education Act*, Oxford: Blackwell.

Part II

Chapter 3

A case study of opting-out
Small Heath School

It was inevitable that the legislation which initiated grant-maintained schools would cause political friction between schools that were attempting to opt out and their maintaining LEA and that the ground rules for the opting out process would be tested in the courts at an early date. The following account by Cecil Knight, OBE, Headteacher of Small Heath School in Birmingham, explores the factors which motivated the governors of his school to call a parental ballot on grant-maintained status and should be read against the wider political backdrop. He describes the process which was followed, highlighting the legal and practical challenges that were encountered and indicating the essential components of such a campaign. Finally, Cecil Knight provides some pointers to what schools must do after a successful ballot and when the Secretary of State gives his approval. Small Heath School was amongst the first eighteen schools to be incorporated as grant-maintained in September 1989.

THE SCHOOL AND ITS SETTING

Small Heath School was formed by amalgamation in 1983 as part of a large scale reorganisation of secondary education in Birmingham, prompted by the need to accommodate falling rolls. It is an 11–16 mixed comprehensive school, set within Birmingham's inner-ring on two sites half a mile apart straddling the main A45 trunk road. The area has one of the highest rates of unemployment in the country and 60 per cent of our pupils are drawn from homes depending on family income support. Over 90 per cent of our pupils are from families originating in New Commonwealth countries. The lower school is set in a century-old listed building which in 1989 was badly in need of modernisation. The upper school is in a modern multi-purpose building incorporating a public library and a sports centre which, during school hours, constitutes its PE facility.

WHY DID THE GOVERNORS SEEK GRANT-MAINTAINED STATUS?

The answer is as complex as the question is simple. The majority of us saw the opportunity to seek grant-maintained status as a positive, proactive, creative response to the challenges which faced us in the autumn of 1988, and which are analysed and explained here.

Competition with outer-ring schools

In the heyday of the Victorian era Small Heath was a suburb created by and for a new generation of successful entrepreneurs, merchants and skilled artisans. Time and Birmingham's continuing expansion have transformed what was once an outer-ring haven for the successful into an inner refuge for many who have not yet made it, but harbour a vision of a better life in the new suburbs. Open enrolment has created a situation in which such aspiring parents may obtain in education what they may not obtain in housing. A tradition has evolved in which pupils tend to travel out to school but never in. Even the city's grammar schools, many of which were originally based in the inner ring, have moved to the periphery. To survive as a school we do not just have to match the performance of our outer-ring colleagues – we have to do better.

The same Act that brought open enrolment also encompassed local financial management, an ineluctable economic force designed to achieve for some LEAs what they were unable to do for themselves: close schools and thus reduce wasteful surplus places. As an inner-ring school with one modern building whose income-generating portions were vested in the council's leisure services committee and another building which promised to become a financial black hole, our potential to thrive appeared tenuous. Add to this that we were approaching the lowest point in the pupil population cycle and were only two-thirds full. The governors thought that a city council with a policy of community education would be acting to safeguard such a key community resource. The governors were dismayed in the autumn of 1988 when the LEA deluged every primary school in our catchment area with full-colour brochures extolling the virtues of our outer-ring competitors – professionally designed publicity commissioned by the LEA that we could not even begin to afford to produce about our school. In addition, such schools already had the built-in advantage of being 11–18 institutions.

Grant-maintained status offered us a chance to fight for better chances in life for our children and a better and more secure future for our community. It offered rewards to the hard-working plus flexibility – the chance to engage in competition on equal terms with our outer-ring colleagues. We asked for no more.

We shared a vision of what we could do with and for our children and our community – given appropriate facilities and resources. While we were justly proud of the measure of success we had achieved, we felt that much of this was in spite of rather than because of LEA support. To have the will but not the means is very frustrating. We studied circular 10/88; we read the articles of the educational economists and the fearful, shallow and unconvincing responses of the administrators; we did our own sums and checked our answers. Grant-maintained status offered opportunities of which we had erstwhile only dreamed!

Priorities! Whose priorities?

What price educational opportunities when your pupils are being denied adequate teaching, books and equipment and being put at risk by falling plaster, penetrating rainwater and soggy wiring? Insofar as we knew that times were hard we sympathised with our LEA, but we felt that funds were being allocated according to a system of mistaken priorities. Frankly we were tired of listening to the ceaseless litanies of 'It can't be done' and 'Don't blame us, blame the government' from politicians and occasionally from officers. Here at last was a golden opportunity for us to set our own priorities and to create our own budget without depriving others. We felt there was everything to gain and nothing to lose.

Aspirations to get on to one site

Anyone who has worked in a split-site school knows the sheer physical effort and stress that is involved in commuting between sites; energy that is wholly wasted as far as any positive educational outcome is concerned. Add to this the increased running costs in terms of maintenance, salaries and duplication of equipment and no one with any sense would support the continuation of such a scenario a moment longer than necessary. It had therefore been one of our main objectives as governors since the inception of the school in 1983 to extend one site so that we could all be together. It seemed to us that the LEA had consistently been unable to take on the true costs of split-site schools, in both financial and educational terms. Further, it had been made crystal clear that as far as capital projects were concerned we could not even aspire to joining the queue. While the governors were not so naive as to believe that grant-maintained status would take us straight to the rainbow's end, we did feel that it would at least enable us to join some sort of queue and at best put us into a position where we might be able to help ourselves by involving investment from outside.

Dynamic relationships

It is not good enough for schools merely to relate to their local communities. There must be such levels of educational, social and economic interchange that both the institution and the environment are in a state of continuous and mutual transformation. Schools are thus not 'knowledge markets'; they only truly fulfil their function when they play their part in changing the world.

Small Heath was once the home of the mighty BSA, whose weapons and machines had indeed contributed to changing the world. With its collapse and the general decline in Birmingham's metal-bashing industries we had become one of the areas of greatest unemployment in the whole of the UK. What does all this have to do with grant-maintained status? On the simplest level, a large school can contribute to its local economy through employment, training and the purchase of goods and services while getting good value for money for its pupils. Further, the very economic nature of this relationship injects a new dynamism into the intercourse between the school and the local community which can only be of benefit to its pupils.

There is a world of difference between being an object of charity and a potential client. For those who had the perception to look beyond the simple mechanisms of grant-maintained status to the impact that it could have upon the whole educational enterprise and to the contribution it could make to the revival of our community a new and exciting prospect presented itself.

The community comes of age?

Grant-maintained status in itself does not create a successful educational enterprise. What counts is using the flexibility and the greater control of resources wisely and purposefully, according to a well-defined educational philosophy. Because by its very nature the educational process involves the mutual support and co-operation of school, parent, child and local community, an educational philosophy that works must arise from a living dialogue between these parties.

For too long the attitude both of local government, whether Labour or Conservative, and of its schools has been unbelievably patronising. To schools: 'You cannot be trusted with your own financial affairs – leave those to us and we will look after you.' To parents: 'Send your children to us and we will do good to them.' In such a situation where the true power remains within the council buildings and within the headteacher's office there can be no genuine co-operation, no meaningful educational dialogue.

While both local financial management and the greater powers and responsibilities of governors were breaking down this ancient system of patronage, grant-maintained status seemed to take that process to its natural conclusion. As a headteacher I take pride in my professionalism and that of my colleagues. By the same token I know that the experience, knowledge and skills which comprise our professionalism cannot operate unilaterally. Grant-maintained status offered a unique opportunity for us all to work in a new and potentially more effective and creative manner.

For many years I had been meeting with local residents' and community groups, sharing my vision of creating a school to which the outer people would want to travel in – part of the renewal of inner-city life. I had always been received courteously, sympathetically but with profound scepticism. Their attitude reminded me of elements from the thinking of that revolutionary educator, Paolo Freire. For him a genuine educational process is enlightening and creative, liberating folk submerged and oppressed within their economic and social environment. Here at last was an opportunity to give real power to ordinary people right at the point of delivery of a key public service: an opportunity for a community to come of age by shouldering its own responsibilities and determining its own priorities albeit within a well defined national curricular framework.

Why call a ballot? Why climb Everest? Because the opportunity and the challenge was there confronting us. Unlike many of the first generation of grant-maintained schools we were not threatened with the push factors of reorganisation or closure. For me and many of my governor colleagues it was the pull factors that attracted us most strongly – in changing times it was time for a change. Schools are of their nature dynamic institutions, always characterised by progression or regression, never merely quiescent. A school that is doing justice to its pupils and its community in our generation must be proactive, goal-oriented and engaged in purposeful, corporate development. That was the kind of school we wanted to create, and grant-maintained status offered an exciting and challenging means of doing so.

THE JOURNEY TO GRANT-MAINTAINED STATUS

Having explained our motivation for setting out I now turn to the journey itself. It was not quite the journey to the Promised Land but the analogy appeals! We were certainly beset by enemies and caused to wonder, like the Israelites of old, whether we would ever have set out if we had been able to anticipate the hazards on the way.

In looking back I recall one of the Beatles' hit songs 'She's Leaving Home'. As I remember, it described the shock to the parents of their daughter leaving home – of coming to terms with the fact that she had come of age and wanted to make a life of her own. This is akin to the reaction of some LEAs when schools wish to seek grant-maintained status. Like some parents they are, on the one hand, hurt and offended and on the other hand, angry because they are losing an asset.

At Small Heath, from the first move we experienced nothing but implacable hostility. The campaign involved the local MPs from whose constituencies the majority of our pupils are drawn. They were supported and assisted by Labour Party councillors, party activists and members of the teaching unions (*Birmingham Post*, 28 November 1988).

The mechanics of the grant-maintained process are described in Chapter 2. The reader's familiarity with the legislation is therefore assumed and the focus is on practicalities.

The first resolution

There are two routes to the ballot which can trigger an application for grant-maintained status: mandate by petition of parents or by governors' resolution. We chose the latter.

In the autumn of 1988 a paper was prepared for the governors explaining the purpose and outcomes of the 1988 ERA. The section on grant-maintained status explained briefly the mode of operation, followed by an analysis of its potential advantages and disadvantages including the greater weight of responsibility that would rest upon us.

The paper was discussed in some detail at the ensuing governors' meeting. All but the two Labour Party representatives agreed that grant-maintained status appeared to offer an exciting and helpful way forward for the school. We interpreted the first vote as no more than a commitment to serious discussion with interested parties and the statutorily required consultation with the council. For us the meeting at which the resolution would be confirmed or rescinded would be the one at which we would make the critical decision. While we hoped for a lively debate, we envisaged that this would take place in the form of direct dialogue rather than at a distance. We were swiftly to be disabused.

After the first resolution

The first vote triggered off a busy round of activities. Immediately on the following morning I telephoned our area education officer to inform him of the decision and of the schedule of meetings that we had arranged in order to listen and consult and to make our second decision. I assured him that we were willing to change the schedule if our proposed dates were not convenient. This was confirmed in writing. It is most important that all conversations should be noted and, where any matter of substance is involved, confirmed by letter. The clerk should further insist that receipt of the letter be acknowledged.

I also informed my colleagues of the decision and of our commitment to listen and consult. We had already circulated information regarding the ERA and had discussed, during a day's teach-in, its implications for our school and ourselves. We ordered a large number of copies of circular 10/88 (Education Reform Act 1988: Grant-Maintained Schools) and distributed them widely. Our aim was to ensure that all interested parties should have as much authoritative information as we could provide.

I also spoke personally and privately to the representatives of teachers' associations and other unions. It was, of course, difficult to say more than that the governors were keen to enable the school to do its very best for pupils and they felt that they must therefore explore every avenue that was available. I tried also to reassure them that, whatever the final outcome, the governors would continue to be concerned to protect them and their jobs.

While this was a time-consuming exercise, during a very busy period of the term, it was vital for the well-being of staff and the efficient running of the school. The prospect of change always tends to generate anxiety. This in turn is heightened when the proposed change is not fully understood and appears threatening. While looking after one's colleagues is a virtuous end in itself, it has also a sound utilitarian justification.

Because our main building was multi-purpose and used for adult education and recreation it was also important to meet with the various managers and to explain the governors' decision to them. At the same time I was able to reassure them both that their interests in the building were protected by law and that the governors were concerned to maintain and enhance the facilities we were pleased to share with the community.

The electoral roll

In anticipation of a possible positive outcome of the second vote we also set in hand the task of drawing up an electoral roll. For us this was a manual operation because we did not have a computerised database. We began with parents of all year 11 pupils. Then we listed parents of all year 10 pupils without siblings in year 11 and so on. Many of our pupils are from Asian families and did not share the same second name. We therefore analysed our pupil population both by family and by address to make sure that particular parents were neither duplicated nor overlooked. It is important to get these matters right first time. Opponents have skilfully exploited mistakes and errors as evidence of duplicity and incompetence.

Meanwhile – the opposition...

While we were busy with the above activities our opponents had not been idle. A carefully planned campaign was about to be launched. It was supported by the local Labour Party and the local MPs from whose constituencies our pupils are drawn. This in itself was evidence of the painstaking attention to strategy that was evident throughout. The local MPs have both worked hard for their constituents and are well respected by our pupils' parents (*Evening Mail*, 14 January 1989, p. 13).

The campaign was characterised by the raising of a series of issues on a weekly basis. One began to scrutinise the *Birmingham Mail* each Thursday and Friday to discover the nature of the next salvo. This is a nationally devised and employed strategy. The same techniques and issues are used almost without exception beginning at the point when governors take the first decision.

Rubbish the governors!

This is salvo one. My influence with parents was noted. Some opponents immediately began to enquire of staff who had known me at various stages in my career if I had committed any professional or personal indiscretions. My first intimations that the campaign had begun came from friends who phoned to warn me that they had been approached. Fortunately I am so boring that they could find no mud to throw. It came as a timely warning of the interest in the case.

Further tactics were to be employed. The campaign leaders sent to the education committee a letter asking it to investigate the legal status of the governing body. They were of course well aware that it was the headteacher who had responsibility for conducting the governing body elections.

I was obliged to send a blow-by-blow account of my actions in minute detail to the chief education officer. This was both intended to be time-consuming, which it was, and to break down morale, which it signally failed to do. This, however, is part of the strategy. It is a little like bombing before lasers. You shower the area in the hope that one will score a hit and in the knowledge that the misses are far from wasted because of the alarm, distress and confusion they cause.

The governors were then accused of causing concern, confusion and anxiety among parents and of being remote and uncommunicative. The truth was, of course, that it was the opponents who had created these anxieties by exposing our alleged subversive plot in the press and over local radio. The governors had decided that the time to inform and consult parents would be following the second resolution to hold a ballot, should it confirm the first.

Buttonhole the parents!

The chief education officer was able to use my statement and evidence from his own departmental records to assure our opponents that we had a validly constituted governing body. I doubt whether they expected any other outcome. The ploy had achieved their purpose of arousing suspicion and creating a publicity base for their campaign.

The next phase was for them to begin approaching the parents in the streets or calling at their homes. The main themes of the opponents' arguments now began to emerge: that the governors were outsiders, who did not really understand local people and local needs; they were interested only in self-aggrandisement; that it was a Conservative plot, and a recipe for bankruptcy; that the teachers would all leave, there would be no more free meals, children would have to pay for recreation, and parents would be asked to pay fees.

My senior colleagues advised me that the rumours had developed to such a degree that it would be better to explain fully to pupils and parents the nature of grant-maintained status, the force of our first resolution and to reassure them that should the final resolution prove positive they would be given detailed explanations and have the last word. After consulting with governor colleagues I wrote to parents and as is our custom on important matters, distributed the letter at year assemblies where a full explanation was given to pupils. Both I and many headteacher colleagues in areas where English is the second language of many parents, and some indeed do not speak English at all, have found that this technique is the best way of getting important messages across.

I wrote out, with great care, what I would say to pupils concentrating on the explanation of the grant-maintained provisions and stressing that there were opposing views which would be fully explored prior to any ballot being held. I made sure afterwards with colleagues whom I knew to be opposed that my presentation had been fair and balanced. It was later to be misrepresented in the media and the courts as part of what seemed to me to be a campaign to undermine trust in my professionalism and integrity.

The consultation with the local authority

We approached the first consultation with the LEA with some trepidation. Whilst we felt we had done our homework, prepared our facts and figures, and planned our strategies for action and development we did not know how they would stand up to the scrutiny of experienced officers.

We need not have worried. The LEA's idea of consultation was to send our area officer armed with a litany of all the woes that could befall the opted out school. For example, it was suggested that positively no company would insure us, that staff would be isolated and unable to attend courses of professional development, that at the first major problem to our building we would be alone and friendless and our pupils without a roof or equipment. There were some minor misconceptions about the services that the LEA would be obliged by law to continue to provide. These and the other threats we gently corrected and countered with what we knew from our research to be the real case. Our colleague was courteously thanked for his presentation and we explored the issues he had raised. We had assumed that the LEA would wish to hold more than one meeting. He was not aware of plans to meet further but would confirm this.

When the governors came to discuss the consultation they concluded that its limited nature only served to confirm the depth of our preparation. They were also concerned about the advice they had received and the extent to which a balanced case setting out the advantages as well as disadvantages had been made. While it served to reinforce the threatening situation into which we had been drawn, it also had the effect of making us all the more determined to proceed – and to win!

Consultations with professional associations and teachers

Because of the exigencies of time we had to limit the amount of consultation in which we could engage. We therefore invited teachers as individuals and through their associations to meet with us and present their points of view. Support staff unions were not invited because their status would not change but, had they approached us, I have no doubt that we would have responded.

We were presented with a wide range of views which were both stimulating and helpful. It was clear that individual teachers and associations were deeply concerned about this new and both threatening and exciting departure from tradition. We were grateful for the thought and care which had been devoted to the presentations and said so.

Consultations with the Grant-Maintained Schools' Trust

The pre-ballot advisory work of the Trust has now been handed over to an entirely separate organisation 'Choice in Education'. The governors invited the director because they wanted to address a range of views for the sake of balance. His presentation was informative, accurate and knowledgeable. He gave equal weight to the advantages and disadvantages and stressed the nature and weight of responsibility that a governing body would need to sustain under grant-maintained status. The governors were impressed by his even-handed approach, his grasp of the facts and his willingness to admit when he was unsure but to seek out the appropriate information and advice.

The second meeting

Following the above period of intense activity, thought and heart-searching the governors met on 14 December 1988 to consider confirming or rescinding the resolution passed on 9 November to hold a ballot.

The LEA had circulated a letter from the CEO and an analytical comparison of the differences between LMS and GMS prior to the meeting. Regrettably it had been sent out so late that most governors had not received it. While some governors were so angered by this inefficiency that they were against considering it, I insisted that it should be copied, circulated and considered in detail. Two officers were present to speak to it. Consequent events caused the governors to be grateful that we had taken this step.

Time has perhaps softened the memory of the emotion of that meeting. We were aware of the powerful forces ranged against us who had vowed to undermine our school if we proceeded. We had no doubt of the intensified controversy we would face if we proceeded to a ballot. (This was recorded in the minutes of the governors' meeting, and in affidavits from Cecil Knight to the High Court, and was not disputed in court.) On the other hand most of us had become convinced of the unique and exciting opportunities that grant-maintained status could provide for our pupils and our community. This same majority were also ready to shoulder the extra burden of responsibility.

The resolution was carried. Our two Labour Party nominated governor colleagues, one of whom was our chairman, voted against, as did another governor. Our two teacher governors abstained to reflect what they considered to be the uncertainty and divided views of their colleagues. We moved immediately to planning the ballot and agreed that it should be conducted from mid-January to mid-February. A small working party, including governors who had been both for and against the ballot, was established to produce a balanced document to send to all parents explaining the issues.

The ballot

After the meeting we confirmed our decision in writing to the LEA and began to make arrangements for the ballot. We then contacted the Electoral Reform Society and agreed dates for the ballot. Because of the multilingual background of our parents we asked for the leaflet explaining grant-maintained status, which by law had to accompany the voting paper, to be sent out in English, Urdu and Bengali – the three main languages among the sixteen which our pupils' parents speak. They later explained that this was impracticable for them. We therefore specified that it should go out in English and that we would make translations available through pupils on request. This decision was later to be challenged in the High Court.

We also compiled our *Additional Information*, informing voters of the names of those who had agreed to become initial governors of the proposed grant-maintained school and we followed the rubric suggested in the DES booklet *How to Become a Grant-Maintained School* (DES 1988, para. 3, annex B). This booklet had now become our bible. Little did we know that our adherence to its advice was to be the subject of actions which eventually took us to the Court of Appeal.

Our balanced document

We then addressed ourselves to producing our balanced document for parents which we hoped to circulate in three languages prior to the Christmas holiday. I wrote a draft which was presented at the working party established at the December governors' meeting. Our chairman failed to attend.

Stop the ballot – or else!

By the end of term the continuing press campaign and the constant interruptions from interested parties to seek explanations had reduced us to a state of near exhaustion. On the penultimate day of term the Education Policy and Finance Committee met. The city solicitor's office acting on behalf of the

LEA had come up with the plea that we had failed to consult adequately with the LEA by not producing in draft the detailed proposals that are required to be published by governors after a successful ballot. To this it subsequently added another plea which arose later in the case of Haberdasher Aske's School: that I, the teacher governors and a parent governor who worked at the school should not have participated in the voting on both first and second resolutions because we had a pecuniary interest.

It is interesting to note that this second plea and later matters that were added were geared to questioning my professional actions and personal integrity. Knowing the bitter opposition we faced from some quarters, had such pleas proved successful, they might have been used as grounds for suspension or dismissal. Fortunately this was not to be the case.

The last day of term arrived. We sent the children home and came together as a staff very much united in our friendship and loyalty to one another and our pupils. At about 5.30 p. m., after the staff had gone home, the phone rang. It was our chairman who sounded surprised to get an answer and particularly from me. He had 'just had a letter placed in his hand' informing the governors that the council would seek an injunction in the High Court unless we cancelled the ballot.

What price freedom?

The city solicitor's letter asked the governors to stop the ballot ... or else. 'If such an assurance is not forthcoming by 9th January I have instructions to take appropriate proceedings in the courts ...' (Birmingham City Council, city solicitor's department).

Our governors were not a group of wealthy people; on the contrary the majority were very much in the lower income bracket. We had no secret backers and there were no promises of finance. To defend ourselves in the courts could be ruinous, and they do not take kindly to losers. On the other hand, to comply with this cleverly timed delaying tactic, for we had no doubt that they had deliberately waited until the Christmas vacation, could be the first step on the path to defeat in a ballot. Compliance would have been used as a sign that we had acted hastily and improperly and were not fit persons to govern an LEA school let alone a grant-maintained school.

A small group of inner-city governors against the might of Birmingham City Council? However, we had been assiduous in following DES advice over the decisions to hold a ballot and the procedures for holding it. We had generated a vision for what we could do for our pupils under grant-maintained status. We sought legal advice and were pointed in the direction of Roger Peach, a solicitor based in Winchester but with a national reputation in education law.

He agreed to meet some of us after Christmas in Oxford, a city unfamiliar to many of our group but thereby serving to heighten our awareness of the struggle in which we had become engaged. He was kindly, understanding, masterly in his grasp of the issues, and he encouraged us to make a stand. Our chairman had not convened a meeting. We exercised our right to convene a meeting, discussed the council's threat, reviewed our actions and the advice we had been given and resolved to press ahead with the ballot. This surprised some, including one or two members of our governing body, who appeared to believe we would back down. Certainly, our chairman did not seem pleased.

Injunctions and ballots

We commenced the new term in a mood of excitement and foreboding. I was deeply moved by the tenacity of my colleague governors, teachers and parents and their willingness to stand against the opposition campaign. Would they carry out their threat of legal action or was it just a bluff? The consequences if we lost were vividly to be conceived in the early hours.

Meanwhile there was work to be done. All the data had been sent to the Electoral Reform Society. Parents had been invited to examine the electoral roll. All but about twenty had asked for their names and addresses not to be released if a request was made. The balanced document from the governors on grant-maintained status had been translated and circulated. The ballot papers would shortly be dropping on parents' doormats and we were faced with a busy round of meetings.

Rather than have one or two large set piece meetings we had decided to run a series of smaller meetings over a seven-day period. This enabled us to make sure that every parent was likely to be able to attend at least one meeting. Many of our parents prefer single-sex gatherings and are happier to ask questions and discuss issues in such a context. We also arranged this facility. Translators were booked so that no one was barred by the language barrier. While all of these measures favoured genuine dialogue they militated against political activists using wrecking tactics. They proved notable for their open exchange of views and the manner in which issues were explored and honestly faced on both sides.

Then, out of the blue, came a message from Roger Peach. The council were indeed seeking an injunction in the High Court. They had obtained the services of an experienced and successful counsel. I hurried to London for a briefing with William Hunter who was to present our case. His infectious humour, his bluff, hearty manner and, above all, his mental agility were to prove sources of encouragement and strength at that first meeting and for months to come.

For me the High Court in the Strand was intimidating, almost threatening, but one nevertheless became caught up in a kind of pre-match excitement. Wilkie, for the council, presented a picture of a group of governors acting in unnecessary haste. Mr Justice Popplewell's response was that the ballot had been properly arranged and could therefore go ahead.

Election campaign

The council had decided not to respond to our invitations to attend meetings of parents. We knew why one Saturday morning when in the same post as the ballot papers every parent received a fat envelope of anti-grant-maintained literature (Birmingham Education Service, n.d.). We met and decided that we had a duty to ensure that parents were enabled to know the facts as we saw them. We had offered to circulate information for the council through the pupils. We therefore felt free to do likewise. At our own cost we produced a series of handbills in English, Urdu and Bengali reiterating the facts. The council had spent nearly £6,000 on their campaign (Birmingham chief education officer, 1989, item 4). The governors phoned and visited. Parents constantly asked 'What does Mr Knight think?' and so I decided to write a personal letter. All of this was later to be described and challenged in the High Court as illegal and unprofessional.

The council then arranged a series of press releases and a special conference for the Asian press. It culminated with the chair of the Equal Opportunities Committee calling for me to be sacked, a matter so serious that it made the headlines in the *Birmingham Mail*. He made his call on the basis of a selectively misquoted passage from an article by me that had been leaked to him which, he claimed, showed unacceptable racial bias. It was in fact a most sympathetic article on some of the issues facing Asian children in Birmingham schools and was freely available in libraries.

In the event the campaign against us and against grant-maintained status failed. We were to win by nearly 100 votes. I believe we won because parents believed what we consistently asserted: we could provide their children with more books, equipment and facilities and better opportunities, and because they perceived our integrity.

More injunctions

Whilst our opponents secretly believed they were winning the ballot – our pupils' parents can make mischief when they are annoyed! – they did not rest. Two of them were to seek an injunction declaring the ballot invalid.

Once again we were brought before Mr Justice Popplewell. The accusations were that I had broken the provisions of the 1986 Education Act by presenting unbalanced political propaganda to my pupils and sought through them to persuade their parents to vote for grant-maintained status. For a time it was not clear that we were to contest these allegations. Mr Justice Popplewell's comments sent a chill down my spine. When it became clear that they were to be contested he ordered them to be struck from the record. The press just missed having a heyday at our expense.

Declarations and proposals

The hearing before Mr Justice Popplewell was on 26 January 1989. The ballot closed on Friday 3 February and we were telephoned with the result on the 6 February. We had waited anxiously to see whether it would make the outcome of our court case academic. From the many kind assurances I had received from parents I was confident of success, except at the bewitching hours between two and four in the morning. Our opponents were equally confident.

Out of 970 parents entitled to vote, 773 had returned papers (79.7 per cent) of whom 435 had voted YES and 338 had voted NO. A sense of elation? Yes, but tempered by the challenge of making grant-maintained status work as we had said it would and the thought of the following month's court case which could still turn victory into defeat. For the time being we busied ourselves with a final look at our proposals prior to publishing them as required and sending them to the Secretary of State. As advised by the DES we kept them short and succinct, taking care to follow the suggested format.

Judicial review

Our case was eventually heard in May and lasted for a week. The opponents sought every possible ground to invalidate the ballot in the hope that at least some might prove valid. We were accused of not properly consulting with the council; participating in discussion and voting when we should have refrained because of pecuniary interest; failing to provide information in appropriate languages; providing insufficient information; participating improperly in the campaign at the time of the ballot; and improperly raising political issues with pupils.

For all that our cause and probably my own career were at stake there were many touches of humour. If I have learned anything from this experience it is that the courts can provide some of the best free entertainment available. The week's wait for the judgment seemed, by contrast, interminable.

Lord Justice Woolf and Mr Justice Kennedy appeared grave and their judgment was long and at times difficult to follow. Then, at one point, Roger Peach turned and smiled, giving a discreet thumbs up. We breathed again. Judgment was entirely in our favour apart from the pecuniary interest issue, on which the Court found that I and my teacher colleagues should neither have participated nor have voted in the discussions on holding a ballot. In their view it had not affected the outcome of the matter and they therefore exercised discretion in our favour and rejected the council's plea that the whole process had thereby been vitiated.

I was both delighted and disappointed. We were all vindicated and more importantly we felt for the first time that we could settle to some serious planning. Yet in another sense I felt our integrity had been impugned. The law on grant-maintained status was clear. The governors would be subject to the same salary regulations as other maintained school governors. We had not stood to lose our jobs by some process of reorganisation. We stood to gain nothing but the satisfaction of doing a better job.

Had the present pay and conditions document been in force, it would have been a different matter. I would now indeed be free to negotiate a salary commensurate with my greater responsibilities.

Secretary of State's decision

We believed the Secretary of State would delay his decision until the council's legal limit for lodging an appeal had passed. Much to our surprise he did not and we duly received his approval in mid-June. We immediately began to make preparations for opening as a grant-maintained school in September. The transitional grant provided our first budget exercise: real power at last.

The council waited until the very last hour of the very last day before lodging their appeal on 27 June. Dennis Howell in parliament and councillors on the council raged against the Secretary of State's temerity in declaring himself before they had decided. Although we had hoped there would be no appeal we were heartened to see that the Secretary of State had now been joined with us in the action. It is comforting to have the company of powerful players in the dock.

The appeal was delayed until the last week in July. We sweltered before Lord Justice Glidewell, Lord Justice Farquharson and Sir Roger Ormrod. The council had secured an outstanding QC to present their case, Elizabeth Appleby. While we remained confident of our trust in William Hunter we admired the skill and elegance with which she made her case.

The pecuniary interest issue turned on a previous case, Bostock and Kaye, in which a headteacher and teacher representatives had voted in favour of a school changing to become a CTC. We laboured hard to demonstrate the significant differences in funding and salary arrangements between grant-maintained schools and CTCs.

The judgment was given on 1 August. The evidence for pecuniary interest was dismissed, which effectively disposed of the appeal. We had now been successful on every accusation brought against us (*Daily Telegraph*, 1989).

I was deeply moved. I had felt that I and my colleagues had until now received the favour of the court, they had exercised discretion in our favour but not their absolution. It had been accepted that there was an element of pecuniary interest in our favour when we voted. While we are far from morally perfect we are not given to that sort of behaviour and would not wish to set that kind of example.

It was then as if not one but two dark clouds had been lifted: the cloud of uncertainty and the cloud of malpractice. After thanking Mr Hunter, I went off with Roger Peach and his partner Janet Gray to indulge in a hearty celebration.

POSTSCRIPTS

And they all lived happily ever after.... Well, not quite. August was a very busy month, negotiating insurance and working with the Assets Board to make an agreement that the council still refuse to ratify. I am grateful for the total loyalty of my colleagues in those services. We now look after these matters in-house to our mutual benefit and that of our pupils. Was it all worth it? Walking around Small Heath, even on a bad day, I can see hundreds of reasons for saying yes, and there are no regrets.

REFERENCES

Abrams, F. (1988) 'Councillors' fear on opt-out move', *Birmingham Post*, 28 November.
Bell, David (1989) 'Opt-out head sack call', *Birmingham Mail*, 20 January.
Birmingham Chief Education Officer (1989) Report of CEO to Education Policy and Finance Committee, 31 January.
Birmingham City Council City Solicitor's Department (1988) letter to Councillor C.J. Eames, 21 December.
Birmingham Education Service (n.d.) *Your Child's School. Your Child's Future.*
Daily Telegraph (1989) 'Teacher governors can vote to change status', 25 September.
DES (1988) *How to Become a Grant-Maintained School*, London: HMSO.
Sparks, S. (1989) 'Roy: opt out of opting out!', *Evening Mail*, 14 January.

Chapter 4

Managing a school and developing a grant-maintained ethos

Roger Perks, Headteacher of Baverstock School in Birmingham provides some thoughts and practical guidance on leadership style and establishing a grant-maintained school ethos. He describes the background to the school and the local community and outlines the reasons why the school opted out. Baverstock School was amongst the first eighteen schools to become grant-maintained in September 1989.

Roger Perks starts from the premise that achieving grant-maintained status does not automatically ensure a good school. He goes on to demonstrate that the opportunities and flexibility it offers provides the means for a school to develop into an effective school.

INTRODUCTION

Baverstock School was formed in September 1983 as an amalgamation of two closing schools, the buildings of which were shared, and the children but not the premises of a third, moving to one site in September 1985. It is situated in the outer-ring of South Birmingham at its border with the county of Worcestershire and Herefordshire and serves the sprawling Druids Heath housing estate. High-rise flats overlook a community which has more than its fair share of deprivation. There is little in the way of an arts heritage and there is no cinema, theatre, nor expansive community facilities. Indeed, were it not for the existence of the school which is at once the focal point and powerhouse of its local community, there would be no real centre for holding the community together or for providing a social base. The relationship of the school to its area is seen by many as positive and mutually beneficial, although there are restrictions regarding the school's ambitions in this direction because of the physical limitations of the site.

It often appears to members of its community that the school was formed as a result of the planners supplying the estate with a newsagents, a public house and a school at its inception in the belief that events would then proceed towards their cyclical conclusion by closure. However, the school, like its estate, has refused to lie down and accept such limitations as lack of a sports hall, playing fields, swimming pool, sixth form, specialist rooms and inferior construction.

In the years which followed its creation, the school grew steadily in popularity rising from four to eight-form entry. In fact, such was the demand for places at the school that by September 1989 all pupils in the school had made it their first choice and the catchment area had grown to include pupils from the opposite end of Birmingham as well as from as far afield as Redditch and Solihull.

In some ways this apparent success of the school militated against its objectives, for there was now a need to share an already thin educational provision among more pupils and teachers within the constraints of the same site. Matters were compounded by an historical underspending on books and materials, by a teacher ratio of one to twenty, by leaking roofs and, principally, by the limitations of the original secondary modern building with its dangerous curtain walling and guillotine-effect windows.

In addition, several rooms, notably those which had served for many years as the traditional models for home economics, metalwork and typewriting were not only out of date and lacking in modern resourcing but were housed in rooms which gave out negative statements to the pupils who used them. The interior of the school, although free from graffiti, was drab, faded, peeling and in many areas actually crumbling.

As a home for the day for our children it lacked style and example. The officers of the LEA had been able to assist in some ways but it was obvious that the scale of the necessary improvements, in terms of health and safety let alone the delivery of the National Curriculum, needed further consideration.

Over a period of time and, certainly, during the two or three years before the opportunity to opt for grant-maintained status arrived, there was a feeling, virtually a belief, amongst most members of the school and local community that the school had been taken as far as it was ever likely to go without a major investment. The arrival of the opt out facility was to present the opportunity for which we were all searching.

SCHOOL LEADERSHIP

Perhaps the first point that should be established is that there is no easy solution, no fail-safe guarantee and certainly no magic wand which will make a failing school into a successful one once it has been endowed with the gift of grant-maintained status. Indeed the Secretary of State for Education has not been minded to approve those schools which believed they could either preserve an already precarious position or become an overnight success through the medium of opting out — a misleading and damaging term if ever there was one. The roots of the real potential for positive improvement and eventual success can be traced to structured systems of educational support which have served existing schools up to the moment of transition.

What is now measurable is that, whilst weak schools can not become strong schools simply by becoming grant-maintained, good schools can become very good ones and the very good schools can become centres of educational excellence. It is also evident that the style of leadership of such a school is inextricably linked to its ethos and development and there is no doubt that the headteacher's position will be both pivotal and crucial.

Thus a relevant and meaningful head would satisfactorily embody the philosophy of Aristotle, the self-belief of Canute, the oratory of Cicero, the classroom teaching of Homer, the communication of Marconi and the leadership of Moses. The head himself would happily settle for a combination of the durability of Mickey Mouse, the escapology of Houdini and the luck of Ronald Biggs.

There are numerous references in the literature to what is required of a headteacher in terms of leadership. White (1984), for example, argues that the priority for inclusion within a training programme for heads is the implementation of 'workplace democracy'. She goes on to say:

> We may, for instance, need radically to revise a common British conception of the school head. Is it appropriate, one might ask, for the head of an educational institution to be the (often) unchallengeable determiner of both major educational policies within the schools as well as the details of the dress of its members? If pupils are faced with this kind of indefensible authoritarianism they are being invited to consider an inconsistency. There is 'talk', as there is in most schools, of democratic ideals and practices, but what pupils actually 'see' is important institutions in society being run on anti-democratic lines.

This is, thank goodness, not often the case in education and it is the leader's role to provide a positive and democratic framework. It is especially important that this applies not only to staff but to each child, so that the child has equal access to resources and a voice in the decision-making process which sets the appropriate mood for the desired school ethos.

Thus, in our way, we point towards the open-ended and heartening nature of working parties, pastoral/academic teams, staff socials, school events, sports teams, school councils, parents' and friends' associations, school-based in-service courses, community liaison, emphasis on problem solving and analysis within the curriculum as well as the comprehensive range of democratic opportunities to be shared in the so-called hidden curriculum.

The school, like society itself, proceeds through consent. To claim a generality of authoritarian, unchallengeable and anti-democratic managerial attitudes is to confess an innocence or even ignorance of general educational practice.

The plain truth is, of course, that a head's style percolates the life and work of the school. From time to time, even the most democratically affected head must make a decision, be it only through the medium of a casting vote. Ask staff, parents, children and members of the local community, whether or not the style of headship is a significant factor in any assessment which is relevant to their respective situations and you will receive a very positive answer. It follows that we cannot afford mistakes at headship level. The destinies of too many people are at stake. Therefore, we must come to terms with training, or at least acknowledge that there are implications during the selection process regarding qualities other than those of an administrative and educational nature which qualify a headteacher for the task of leading a school and building the necessary ethos.

ESTABLISHING A SCHOOL ETHOS

Although the transition to a grant-maintained school is not necessarily a quantum leap forward, there should nevertheless be an understanding that there are significant changes in approaches which need to be addressed, some, such as financial guidelines, through training, and others such as market awareness, through instinct. A reading of the Education Reform Act 1988 will have sent the pulses racing and the adrenalin flowing as the reader became enthused with the prospect not only of converting educational opportunity into reality, but also of taking a successful LEA school like Baverstock into another dimension of educational experience as Baverstock Grant-Maintained School.

It is at such a point that the leadership of a school is required to articulate its educational philosophy in clear and precise terms. If that philosophy is acknowledged as directed towards and centred around the children themselves and is ambitious for their personal, academic and social achievement, those concerned in its implementation will be more confident of its eventual success. Within this context the move towards grant-maintained status for Baverstock was never seen as a political gesture but as an educational opportunity. By the time minds had been made up and hearts won over, the school was ready to take a calculated view of its capability and potential delivery.

An audit now needed to be undertaken with regard to personal strengths and weaknesses, not least of which would be the coming to terms with managing a situation with increased responsibilities for finance, administration, support services, in-service training and planning. At the heart of the matter lay the certain belief that the face-to-face relationships built up over a period of six years – and surely the prime reason for the success of the school – should be preserved at all costs despite the potential increase in organisational duties. Therefore, there was a realisation that there were considerable implications in terms of time, priorities and even lifestyle, however counterbalanced these might be by a reduction in the customary levels of frustration when dealing with the various aspects of an extended bureaucracy.

By the time that we had received notification that we were to become the first school in the Midlands to have our proposals for grant-maintained status accepted by the Secretary of State, we were well advanced with our preparations, not least because, although we had heard on 6 February 1989 that the Secretary of State was 'minded to approve' our submission, objections had been raised regarding the proposed intake of 240 children. Therefore, before the final confirmation on 12 May 1989, decisions had already been taken regarding the crucial areas of managerial input, staffing, both teaching and ancillary, the scope and breadth of the curriculum as well as the composition of the new governing body. In the crucial area of teacher provision, for example, we had decided that we needed six teachers over and above our existing allocation, that they should all be specialists and that any further vacancies would be advertised nationally, in order to create the academic ethos which we were determined to further. In addition, we would increase our secretarial component from three to six and would appoint a bursar, with additional help to take the place of the city council's administrative machinery.

Once the glad tidings about grant-maintained status were received our school plans were not only reconsidered but also modified and sharpened in the light of events as they unfolded. Each decision was taken having regard to preserving and strengthening the existing ethos of the school and the priority with such issues was the preservation of the human face and form of the school.

In such a context, therefore, it would have been inappropriate for the head and members of the senior management team to have become involved in the administration and minutiae of financial returns, or for valuable setting-up time to be eroded on those duties for which we could employ additional secretarial help from our transitional grant. At the same time, it was most appropriate that such colleagues would be significantly involved in the management of those areas as well as in the establishment of any committees or working parties.

In fact, during the last two months of the summer term before incorporation not only were we holding meetings of the existing governing body but also preparing the way for the incoming governing body. With regard to the latter, it was decided to establish six sub-committees which would be of a consultative nature reporting back to the full governing body. These sub-committees focused on pupils, to include admissions and appeals, curriculum, staffing, buildings, repairs and maintenance, marketing and finance. They represented a key element in the preparation for a new atmosphere in the school. Members of the senior management team according to their experience and expertise joined each of these committees so that there was never any danger of education being dissociated from the business side of affairs and, by the same token, governors could be involved from the very dawn of the new era as well as being in a position to receive information and furnish advice at first hand.

At this stage in the school's development there were six members of the management team all of whom had a role to play, in terms not only of their school duties but also of involvement with the grant-maintained element. Examples of these additional roles included the following areas: the first deputy had responsibility for communication to which was added the grant-maintained dimension of the marketing and sponsorship brief; the second deputy, having an overall pastoral responsibility, became associated with building, repairs and maintenance; the third deputy who carried responsibilities for curriculum and INSET had additional oversight of capitation and resources; and the two senior teachers with responsibility for examinations and pupil development picked up TVE and employees' contracts respectively.

There was a need to commit to the written word our aims for Baverstock as a grant-maintained school. The initial aims were framed as follows:

1 for the highest possible standards of personal and social behaviour and academic achievement;
2 for all members of the school community to be happy, feel valued and be able to influence the direction and atmosphere of the school;
3 to provide a caring environment in which each child is easily locatable, has a point of contact or reference, feels valued, supported and essential to the on-going programme, in which the work ethic is seen to be an important and integral part;
4 to provide a well-balanced, relevant curriculum and a broad experience of extra-curricular activities, thus helping to ensure that each pupil has the maximum opportunity for personal development;
5 to recognise the individuality of each pupil with reference to his or her particular needs, helping to ensure that education is able to fit him/her for life with all its challenges, problems and achievements;
6 to recognise positively all progress, attainment and effort;
7 to make the school a focal point of the local area and community and to involve parents and other members of that community in the co-operative task of preparing each child to become a responsible contributor to a changing society;
8 to have serious regard for the educational continuum, fostering relationships with 'feeder' primary schools and 16+ providers;
9 to be committed to the promotion of equality of opportunity for all pupils with due regard to race, gender and disability;
10 to make our pupils aware of the challenges, opportunities and realities of life after school;
11 to deal with issues affecting the education of children with idealism and, hopefully, with vision.

Although such reactions to rapidly developing circumstances were sometimes framed in a considered manner they were at other times, it must be confessed, conceived somewhat spontaneously. An ordered and orderly programme of planned, sequential development was urgently needed in order to rationalise and articulate our projected requirements. Only then would we be able to ensure that our school's ethos could be established on sound foundations and its roots set in tablets of educational stone.

SCHOOL DEVELOPMENT PLANNING

It was decided that a school development plan should be fashioned which would not only satisfy those identifiable criteria designed for short-term planning but also encompass our projections as the school developed over the next five and, possibly, ten years. At the same time and hopefully running in parallel would be our performance indicators, the results and revelations of which would help us monitor the developing situation as well as to measure the extent of any strengths and weaknesses. Accordingly we produced the following schedule of events:

Summer 1989   Draft copies of the school development plan and performance indicators produced, distributed and discussed.

September 1990 Using DES performance indicators *aide-memoire* as a base, a first statistical return produced.

October 1990   Staff supplied with a copy of this statistical return, together with a questionnaire concerning strengths/weaknesses of the school. These two to be used as a school audit.

November 1990 The details of the questionnaire produced – staff in small groups on INSET day to produce short/mid/long-term targets together with appropriate means of monitoring and evaluating its success (performance indicators).

Jan/April 1991 Development plan placed before the middle management committee for ratification/amendment.

Summer 1991   Final discussions and assessments.

September 1991 Plan commences in the following manner:

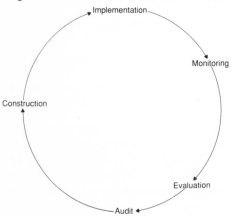

A NEW START

On 5 September 1989 the doors of the former Baverstock School were opened to the first intake of grant-maintained children. It was to be a celebration of 'GM' with GM ties, button, blazer and jumper badges, even GM mugs as well as Gardner Merchant who were organising our catering and making their own 'GM' contribution.

There was a great deal of media interest especially as there were only eighteen schools in England and Wales who were able to call themselves grant-maintained. The atmosphere was one of excitement, anticipation and, for some, apprehension. Most people remember that first day as a positive and inspiring occasion. People who knew the school well and appreciated its highly structured programmes of support were in no doubt that the school would be a resounding success; certainly, the announcement regarding the over-subscription for the new intake was treated as a vote of confidence in the new school – 241 for 240 places.

Moreover the school's place in educational history was to be effectively chronicled by the media. An early visitor was Paul Marston from the *Daily Telegraph* who wrote on Thursday 7 September 1989:

> For the school walls, opting out has proved rather a shock. Many are receiving their first lick of fresh paint since they were built 20 years ago, and in one school a wall in the dining hall was demolished within hours of earning the new catering manager's disfavour. Flexibility of action is already reality at Baverstock School, one of the first wave of schools to open its doors this week under grant-maintained status, directly funded by the Department of Education and outside local authority control.

Significantly, he became immediately aware of the structures necessary for long term success:

> Other old-fashioned virtues prevail. Since long before last year's legislation on collective worship, the school has held an assembly every morning, with a hymn and the school prayer, and Armistice Day is marked each year with a visit from a British Legion marshal and six standard-bearers.

As the school settled into its new routine other interested visitors arrived including Melanie Whitehouse and Declan Cunningham from the *Daily Express* who, under the heading 'Go-it-alone school that is in a class of its own', observed the following:

> A school which ought to be a failure has turned into a resounding success – with both pupils and teachers queuing to get in.
>
> Despite its unpromising surroundings – it sits in the middle of a sprawling high-rise housing estate – almost 1,000 parents whose children leave junior schools next year turned up at an open evening last week.
>
> Within half an hour, all 240 places available for the next school year were snapped up.

Competition for 10 teaching places was even tougher, with an amazing 300 applications.

By the time February 1990 arrived the school had passed through one full term without disaster and received the education team from the *Sunday Times* who arrived hard upon the ministerial heels of Angela Rumbold following her visit to Denmark. She was reported as being interested in the radical approach of the Danes to education and their perceived demands for competitiveness and accountability:

> Almost 700 miles away at Baverstock School, Birmingham, her vision of a better future is being put into action. The motto, 'Strive to Succeed' is emblazoned over a battered blue door which cannot have seen a new coat of paint in years.
> Situated on the Worcestershire border, next to a high-rise overspill estate, the school has struggled to provide a better future for its under-privileged pupils. Its buildings bear the hall-marks of the 1960s building boom: flat roofs that need replacing at a cost of £250,000; facades which are coming away from the walls and will cost £270,000 to repair.

By the summer term the school was seen by both its customers and the media as something of a fixture. The *TES* in its news focus was able to report on the pride of Baverstock's pupils:

> Baverstock School in Birmingham, newly opted out, has revamped its already strict uniform with a new tie embroidered with the letters GM and this is also worn on blazers. The ties and badges are sold in the new 'Bavershop' on the school premises and it is all part of emphasising the new grant- maintained status.

These were sentiments which were examined in greater detail by the *Times Educational Supplement* in May 1990:

> Pupils at Baverstock School in Birmingham are so taken back by their school's newly-gained grant-maintained status that they write the initials GM on everything from exercise books to satchels. . . .
> 'Our children have a markedly improved self-image in an area which has the highest number of referrals to the social services in Birmingham', said Mr Roger Perks, the school's headteacher.

Keeping pace with these developments was the school prospectus which was published in full colour and which sought to acquaint potential customers as well as interested people from the area and beyond with the details of the school's formation, its accommodation, catchment area, as well as its aims. In addition, a brief explanation about grant-maintained status was furnished as well as details of pupil organisation, school curriculum, examinations, award and reward system, extra curricular activity, work within the community, school organisation, staff organisation and structure, the role of the school in multicultural society, the Baverstock School Association, the governing body and of course the school rule:

BAVERSTOCK GRANT-MAINTAINED SCHOOL RULE

TREAT ALL PEOPLE IN OUR SCHOOL AS YOU WOULD LIKE THEM TO
TREAT YOU AND OUR SCHOOL WILL BE A VERY HAPPY ONE

DEVELOPING A PARTNERSHIP

All members realise the individual and collective responsibilities which such a rule demands and expects of them. The tone and style of the brochure supports the school's own statements of quality assurance and finesse of presentation with suitable accompanying photographs showing involved and interested pupils taking an active part in the life of their school.

Yet perhaps the greatest beneficiaries and indeed advocates of the GM style are to found in those aspects of the organisation which reflect the human element. Thus, for example, when teachers discover that significant amounts of resources are ploughed into the classroom in terms of books, materials and appropriate equipment, pupils will benefit from having at their own disposal the relevant technology as well as the means of effecting short and long term delivery, whilst parents will be more aware of the localised and national input into the education service. When pupils find themselves affected by the improvement in the shared classroom performance because teachers are able to receive their rightful and appropriate in-service training, parents will feel more confident regarding the quality of educational provision as the National Curriculum is developing.

When parents, witnessing and testifying to this positive and exciting demonstration of real and potential educational excellence become actively involved, not merely with fund-raising events but by pledging skills and supporting teachers and pupils both in and out of the classroom, then the teachers themselves will be both encouraged and further supported at the various points of delivery. In addition, the pupils will now begin to comprehend that there is a conspiracy of support in which they are the desired objective. In such an equilateral triangle of vested interests there can be no one side which is either weaker than or less supportive to the remaining two sides.

In educational folklore one or two of these groups (pupils, parents and teachers) have tended to see the other group as at worst, being openly or secretively hostile, or at best as providing an obstacle to the fulfilment of their own perceived objectives. When the grant-maintained ethos has been effectively established and because each side of the educational triangle is further strengthened by an on-site, on-the-ball governing body, each member is conscious of an additional dimension of personal and professional support.

However, one speaks of establishing an ethos for a grant-maintained school it is an undeniable fact that the maintenance and furtherance of such an ethos needs to be continually supported, and that the most effective means of support is in the improvement of the daily lot of pupils and staff.

SCHOOL IMPROVEMENT

After two years of independence the school was able to claim through a written self-assessment the following improvements within its own context:

Pupils

As well as the improvements regarding their access to improved capitation, increased teacher-to-pupil ratio, ancillary staff, parental involvement and an aesthetically more pleasing 'home for the day', our children have a markedly improved self-image in an area which has the largest number of referrals to social services in the city. The City of Birmingham Social Services Department, Centre 11 area office report for 1983 stated:

> In the view of Centre 11 Social Services and a number of other welfare agencies two sub-areas of the ward of Brandwood demonstrate and display social characteristics more reminiscent of areas located within the inner city.
>
> Levels of deprivation experienced within the ward are characterised by a high degree of spatial concentration. In respect of this, the Dawberry Road and Druids Heath areas have 'attracted' and absorbed a considerable range and volume of welfare resources.
>
> In common with a number of other outer-city neighbourhoods, the profile area 'patches' have not been accorded the status of priority areas within the City's major resource allocation programmes.

Despite such surroundings as high-rise flats and estate land, the school has been able to improve still further its position as a focal point and powerhouse of the local community, so that pupils, parents and local people use the facilities during most evenings. There has been a consequent increase in the number of clubs/activities and social functions.

Capitation (books and materials)

- 1 September 1989 – departmental allowances increased by 50 per cent for National Curriculum and 30 per cent for other subject areas.
- Increased general capitation of 300 per cent in the first year and 600 per cent since.

Staffing

A further 6 teachers appointed over LEA provision, together with two special educational needs specialist teachers and an assistant for modern languages.

INSET

In-service training in school is administered by the deputy head with responsibility for the curriculum and the staff development committee, which comprises the aforementioned deputy, a senior teacher with responsibility for probationers, TVE co-ordinator, representatives from the heads of department and heads of year meetings as well as a classroom teacher representative. In our second year we managed a budget of £43,000 for in-service training provided through the SPG(D) which outlines the priorities for spending. The national priorities are school management and National Curriculum, although the school is able to highlight its own local priorities.

The school was extremely fortunate in acquiring the services of Solihull LEA for the major part of its provision and has full access to Solihull's programme which has been instrumental in providing National Curriculum advice and training to heads of department, in addition to other areas such as probationary teachers support. Moreover, Solihull's team of inspectors has provided a regular and highly valued programme of visits to the departments in order to monitor, evaluate and offer advice.

Ancillary staffing

The administrative/secretarial provision has been increased to seven members – who, in effect, take the place of LEA support officers – as well as the appointment of a full-time school nurse (no former provision) and in-house cleaning services. All employees from the canteen and catering services (contracted out) remained with the school, with the exception of the catering manageress. The number of children staying for school dinners is now 920 as opposed to 400 with the LEA canteen. A second science technician has been appointed.

Intake

The number of applications for places over each of the past two years as a grant-maintained school shows an increase of over 300 first choice applications.

Internal improvements

We have changed the character of two rooms creating a sports science centre from an outdated metalwork room and a restaurant/home economics training centre from an outmoded cookery room. Also in the area of craft, design and technology an extractor fan system has been installed as well as a chipping forge and technical desks. Classrooms have been carpeted as well as new furniture being purchased, new shelving units have been put up in the library.

In addition we have refurbished the Great Hall, installing a new stage, sound and lighting effects, curtains and safety measures. We have also painted stairwells, improved furnishings and created a school shop and music practice rooms from unused areas. During last year's summer holidays we created a further three classrooms and revamped the suites of the heads of year and secretaries.

External improvements

After 20 years of LEA control there are, of course, areas which need urgent attention with regard to health and safety and, indeed, the National Curriculum. Despite this, we have improved the external appearance of the school by putting new school signs over main entrance doors, replacing fencing and enriching the environment around the school, such as external decoration, renewing the roof, new curtain walling on the middle block as well as installing four portakabins.

Governing body

Since the governing body, head and senior management team have been able to prioritise and manage resources, we have been able to make considered decisions about the short and long term needs of the school. This has resulted in savings in repairs, maintenance and improvements.

Applications for teaching posts

For every vacancy, in each subject area, there has been an increasing response from a national field, so that even in the areas of science and mathematics we have not only been able to employ the required number of specialists, but have even turned away teachers.

Parental involvement

There has been a marked increase in active parental support for the school, including weekend painting and decorating parties pledging and furnishing such skills as carpet-laying and plumbing, as well as gardening and general tidying-up groups. Parents now feel that, as the school prayer says, *This is our school*. May all who dwell here live happy together.'

Community links

One of the advantages in building and retaining an ethos of a grant-maintained school lies in the nearness of the governing body to the immediacy of the school situation, especially when a whole school approach is the favoured model. Our governors have set about this in three main ways: first, through informal visits which may take the form of attendance at school functions, discussing over refreshments or simply by calling in at school matters which are not necessarily of great pith and moment; second, through using the head, members of the senior management team or teacher governors to communicate ideas and information; and third, through the various sub-committees. It is a source of continuous amazement and delight that governors are able to attend so many meetings and put so much good sense into the school while still pursuing their own interests and careers. Perhaps they too have been enthused by the atmosphere of the school but perhaps they too believe that their actions are enhancing the lives of the pupils and staff for whom they are ultimately responsible.

The underlying concern of head and governors is that all colleagues, whether they be part of the teaching, bursarial, secretarial, supervisory, caretaking, catering, nursing or, indeed, any member of the support staff, should feel properly valued for their real contribution to the work and life of the school. Certainly, as this concern has been progressively effected, the clear message of team work and shared aims has not been lost upon the younger and more impressionable members of our school.

Finally, it must be stated that an integral part of the school's ability to foster and sustain its own unique ethos is rooted within its regard for certain traditional virtues and values. Therefore, although real and serious regard is paid to the religious and cultural identities of people from a whole range of ethnic and special groups through the media of such agencies as religious education, personal, moral and social education, history and geography, as well as through the so-called hidden curriculum, the school's Christian ethos has been further articulated, as, for example, during morning assemblies where, despite a range of hymns being sung, one in particular has become known as the 'School Song'.

REFERENCE

White, P. (1984) *School Management: A Case for Workplace Democracy'.*

Chapter 5

Managing finance in a grant-maintained school

Keith Barker, Headteacher of Queensbury School in Dunstable, describes his school's first attempts at managing its own budget. Queensbury School became grant-maintained in September 1989 and, as Bedfordshire was not involved in the LMS pilot schemes, there was no such experience within the school. The school's main source of funding, the annual maintenance grant, was based on the school's historical costings and there was considerable dispute over it between the LEA and the school.

Keith Barker writes an honest account of the difficulties and issues that concerned him and his governors at this time, as well as indicating the changes that they have made in the light of this experience.

INTRODUCTION AND BACKGROUND

This chapter should not be read as a treatise on the financial management of grant-maintained schools but as the faltering steps of a school moving overnight from a capitation of £40,000 to a budget of £1.5 million. Such a dramatic change does not have to send shockwaves through the school's organisational system but it certainly exposes some cracks. It will become clear that these cracks need not be serious. Indeed, they can be beneficial because they give a constant reminder that no matter how good a system we think we might have, there is always room for improvement.

Since the first grant-maintained schools were incorporated, there has been another provision of the 1988 ERA implemented that has had a significant effect on many of the remaining LEA schools. The advent of Local Management of Schools (LMS) has enabled most schools to manage an increasing amount of their own budget. The larger secondary schools and sixth-form colleges have budgets greater than many grant-maintained schools so there is increasing expertise in handling large sums of money. However, LEA-maintained schools do not have the same level of financial freedom as schools that are grant-maintained. Few of them yet have cheque-book access to spend their total budget, process their invoices or actually pay the salaries and deal with tax and national insurance. Nor do they have total freedom in placing contracts. Much of the management of the financial transactions is still done by the LEA. Nevertheless, the experience of LMS will take a prospective grant-maintained school a long way down the path of total financial management.

EARLY PLANNING

A school needs to plan the reality of going grant-maintained at the same time as it prepares the application. For financial purposes there are two appropriate starting dates: 1 April and 1 September. The former marks the beginning of the financial year and makes a clean start for financial administration. The latter has the advantage that the school becomes grant-maintained at the beginning of the school year, although this date does mean that the school operates under two different systems in one financial year. January 1 seems to give the worst of all worlds. The choice of date will need to be one of the early decisions made during the preparation of the school's proposal.

Another consideration to be made at this stage is the timing of the appointment of a bursar. For many schools there seems to be an immediate assumption that, because large amounts of money are involved, the early appointment of a bursar is necessary. At Queensbury we made this assumption and found to our cost that it had been inappropriate at that stage.

Perhaps the first question should be: What are the tasks and assets that the governors are responsible for under grant-maintained status? It is worth drawing up a list of all the responsibilities and actions needed and then prioritising them. It will soon become clear that there is more to running a grant-maintained school than managing the money. The governors are responsible for an educational business, and business organisation is essential.

Having listed the tasks, bearing in mind that the list is never closed, the current staffing situation should be considered next. Identify the members of staff who are able to carry out each task and add these names to the list. Use a further column, headed 'training', to indicate training requirements and potential. It is recommended that this exercise is carried out with all teaching and non-teaching staff, so that all available expertise is considered. It is also likely that this exercise will have identified further tasks, hence the remark that the task list is never closed.

The next move is to look at the tasks and see if they can be naturally grouped. Areas of responsibility will begin to evolve together with appropriate members of staff to take them on. Gaps will also become obvious and a recruitment/training plan will need to be drawn up. It is at this stage that contracts for certain services such as grounds maintenance, cleaning, school meals and payroll need to be considered. However, a prospective grant-maintained school will find that it is not short of firms offering their services in all of these areas, as well as other services not previously considered. There is no need for the school to fear that it will be without these services if it decides not to manage them from within.

The reader should take the foregoing as a cautionary tale and one learnt from experience. At Queensbury we did not carry out this analysis at the start and went straight ahead with the appointment of a bursar to an ill-defined post. The venture was doomed from the start and did not last long. Having learnt from the experience we carried out a task identification and an analysis of the skills and competencies of every person employed at the school and came up with different criteria and an entirely different post. We discovered that many of our non-teaching staff could carry out the administrative functions which we had considered beyond them and that we had a wealth of experience amongst the teaching staff which we had hardly tapped. However, from the outset we retained our caretaking, cleaning and school meals staff and, as grounds maintenance was already out to contract, the contractors were retained.

It is also worth knowing the skills and expertise that exist within the governing body. The task identification method can be used to identify these as well as any skills that it would be useful to obtain from future governor appointments. It may emerge that some gaps in the staff analysis can be adequately filled by governors, thus avoiding unnecessary appointments or costly specialist help.

So far, little has been said in this section specifically about finance, yet everything mentioned has to do with money. Every person employed, every service contracted out, every odd job done by an outsider is a cost to the school which means that this money cannot be used elsewhere. The whole basis of the task analysis is to see who should be appointed to do what particular task, and which tasks should be contracted out. A caretaker who cleans windows will save the school the cost of a window-cleaning contract but possibly at the expense of a carpenter to mend or change door locks and a plumber to repair the toilets. The staff analysis will make it clear what can be done by those already employed at the school and what posts have to be advertised. It will also assist in the preparation of job descriptions. Only then can the school ask: 'Do we need a bursar?'.

Let us assume that the appropriate people have been identified. Accommodation needs to be considered next. If people are to carry out their functions properly they need bases from which to work and the appropriate facilities and resources. Many schools have woefully inadequate office space, whether it be for individuals or small groups. It might require a radical review of the physical organisation of the school to address these issues, but such a review must be done and costed. Again, early planning means that, when the time comes, the alterations can be carried out with the minimum of fuss.

THE TRANSITIONAL GRANT

Many of the needs identified in the early planning can be funded from the transitional grant. The early planning will have identified the staffing, accommodation, equipment and training needs which must necessarily be in place before incorporation. The transitional grant can be used to meet all of these, together with the salaries plus on-costs of any additional administrative staff employed as part of the transitional process. The employment of these additional members of staff in itself produces an immediate problem, since they are employed by the school, not the LEA, and the school is responsible for paying them. This means that the school needs to put into place all the necessary employer procedures, for example, ensuring that the Inland Revenue knows about their change of employer. Payrolling will be dealt with in detail in a later section but it is worth mentioning here that if the school is not going to operate its own payroll system, tentative arrangements should be made with a payroll agency at the time of submission to the DES. This will also speed up negotiations once the approval has been granted and the cost can be included in the transitional grant application.

Many schools will already have computers for administration but their adequacy and compatibility need to be considered. IBM compatible PCs of the 386 series are recommended but the numbers needed and whether or not they should be networked (I would recommend that they are), will be a decision for each school. The number of machines will also be influenced by the accounting method to be used, particularly if the school is running its own payroll. A separate, non-networked machine, housed in its own office, is required if the school intends to operate an accounts/payroll package. It is vital that the accounts cannot be accessed from other terminals since this might leave the system open to fraud. Additionally, the operator needs peace and quiet in which to work. A fully equipped work station licensed to run with word-processing and spreadsheet packages, can cost up to £30,000; accounting and payroll packages are priced accordingly.

The amount of training required will depend upon the extent to which people are learning new or extending existing skills. At Queensbury, we have found that the most beneficial training has been given by the trainer coming to the school rather than by sending colleagues away. Not only is it more cost effective, but also there is a greater feeling of practical relevance when it is done at the place of work. In all of this, it is important not to forget the governors. It is easy to identify training needs amongst staff but governors also need some help with their new responsibilities. Thankfully, the advent of LMS has prompted many LEAs to train governors and this will certainly help them take on full responsibility under grant-maintained status. However, some governor training for grant-maintained status is likely to be necessary and should be budgeted for.

In this section I have highlighted key areas of expenditure at the transitional stage and ways in which the grant can be used effectively. The total amount of the transitional grant does not have to be spent between approval and incorporation; many of the invoices will not be received during that time and it is doubtful if all the training will be completed. However, early planning and calculation of what is required from the transitional grant will enable the school to prepare the claim so that an immediate response is possible at the time of the announcement of the school's approval for grant-maintained status.

DES FINANCIAL GUIDELINES

It is appropriate, before moving on to the annual budgetary process, to begin by looking at the guidance given by the DES on financial management. The weighty tome, known colloquially as the 'rainbow pack' because it comes in white, yellow, pink and pale blue sections, was first issued as financial circular letter (FCL) 1/89. This has since been superseded by FCL 7/90 and FCL 7/91, and each revision has made the reporting requirements slightly less onerous.

As a fairly regular traveller at weekends on the West Coast main line to Edinburgh to watch Hearts at Tynecastle or rugby at Murrayfield, I had the bright idea that reading this treatise might be a good way of passing the time during the journey. Not that I needed any help. My own interest in railways and the superb scenery north of Preston meant that every journey was absorbing. However, with good intent I boarded the train at Milton Keynes and settled down to read. The sheer momentum of something new meant that I had read the white section by Rugby and was well into the yellow section, although wilting, by Crewe. Such was my stimulation that I was able to appreciate the delights of the suburbs of Wigan as the pages slipped from my grasp! Clearly my intentions were misplaced because I could respond to anything if it was a distraction from reading the rainbow pack. Such indiscipline would not do and I reckoned, this time more accurately, that with darkness on the return journey and a Hearts victory to fortify the spirit I would find reading much easier.

Applicants for grant-maintained status should not wait for approval before reading this circular letter or its successors. It is advisable to obtain a copy from another grant-maintained school or the DES as soon as possible and begin to take action on its contents. It is likely that further additions to the task list established in your early preparations will emerge but, more importantly, the contents of FCL 7/91 provide a great deal of guidance and answer many questions. At some stage, sooner rather than later, everyone connected with the financial administration of the school will have to read, mark, learn and inwardly digest the contents of the rainbow pack and for this reason it may be appropriate to obtain a summary of it from a professional accountant or similar person.

The white section

This can be briefly dismissed because it contains the covering letter plus amendments to previous FCLs. This section is of importance to existing grant-maintained schools because, by highlighting the changes, they are able to go quickly to the relevant sections without having to plough through every word to discover, or more likely miss, these changes.

The yellow section

This section, entitled 'Financial Memorandum', covers the responsibilities of the governing body and the actions which it must take to ensure proper financial procedures are kept:

The governing body shall designate a Responsible Officer, who need not be a governor, in particular to:

(a) advise it on the discharge of its responsibilities under this Memorandum;

(b) ensure the efficient, economical and effective management of its resources and expenditure, including funds, capital assets and equipment, and staff;

(c) ensure the introduction and maintenance of sound internal financial controls;

(d) seek to ensure that financial considerations are taken fully into account in reaching decisions and in their execution; and

(e) be responsible for signing, with the Chairman of the governing body, its annual accounts, ensuring they are properly presented and causing records to be maintained relating to the accounts.

This extract illustrates the importance which every governing body should place on this post. The paragraphs are explicit but the best person to carry out these duties may not be so obvious. In some schools, the headteacher may have been designated the Responsible Officer; in others, it is the bursar or equivalent person who fulfils this role. At Queensbury, we made the decision that it should be someone who had no direct involvement in the financial affairs of the school. This immediately cut out every person employed at the school, the chairman and vice-chairman of governors, and the governor directly involved in financial management of the school's affairs. Our Responsible Officer is another governor who is able to give impartial and independent advice and may come into the school at any time to inspect the books, examine the systems and ask questions (because he has no vested interest in what he sees or hears other than as a member of the governing body). The DES is very keen on the separation of responsibilities and duties, rightly so as large sums of public money are involved. We felt that this principle should be clearly followed at Responsible Officer level.

The blue section

Guidelines on financial systems and controls appears as the last section of FCL 7/91, yet I feel it should follow the yellow section so I shall deal with it next. This is really the day-to-day operational guidelines of financial controls and all related systems.

It contains a wealth of guidance and advice for any school managing a budget. It also deals with computer-based accounts systems and the problems which these can create. To attempt to summarise its contents would do an injustice to their importance. If the content seems overwhelming, it should be remembered that it is not necessary to implement everything instantly and that the preparation of many of the procedures required can be allocated to different people. It is necessary for a school to draft its own financial procedures and, importantly, these drafts should be exchanged between writers so that clarity and understanding can be tested. The task of setting up the procedures is never finished as amendments may become obvious as they are tested out or as the DES requires them.

This is where the word processor comes into its own. Amendments which might be only a word or a sentence or the insertion of a new paragraph can so easily be made. For this reason, each procedure should begin on a new page so that it can be easily changed without a major revision to the complete text. If each procedure is dated the changes are easily made and the procedures manual is kept up to date.

The pink section

Financial reporting and annual accounts requirements deals in detail with the basis of the financial returns which have to be made to the DES. It provides useful information for preparing budgets and gives the DES an opportunity to monitor on a regular basis whether or not the school's financial affairs are being managed properly. There are six financial returns, three of which are due prior to the start of the financial year, one due monthly, another due quarterly and the final one, the audited accounts, are due by 31 August following the end of the financial year. Any school which fails to meet the reporting requirements may have its annual maintenance grant withheld. Again, this is a section which would be of interest to LMS schools.

THE BUDGETARY PROCESS: FINANCIAL YEAR 1990–1

The budgetary process has two elements. The first, and main part, deals with the annual maintenance grant which provides the bulk of the money for the school. The second deals with much smaller amounts which come in the form of bids for specific items of expenditure.

Element one – budgeting and the annual maintenance grant

When dealing with the annual maintenance grant and other subsidiary grants it is necessary to have a clear view of the budgetary process. The first priority must be to ensure that staff are paid. It is a sobering start to know that salaries will account for over seven-tenths of the total budget. At Queensbury we began to use the freedom of managing our own budget by doubling the amount allocated traditionally to capitation items and spent a little on brightening the main public areas of the school with a coat of paint. Despite this, on the face of it little appeared to have changed financially from LEA days. The governors' caution was understandable. However, as the first financial year progressed, they became more flexible as it became evident that we were solvent and likely to end the year with a healthy surplus.

During the Christmas holiday 1989 a colleague and I spent some time preparing our first formal draft of a budget. Although this may appear to be rather late in the year, the reason for this can, once again, be traced back to the ill-defined bursarial post. To compound our problems, we had not received at this time any indication from the DES about our AMG for the following year. We took the cautious view that there would be a 3 per cent increase on the full-year equivalent to the grant we had received during the first seven months of grant-maintained status and we then rounded down to the nearest £10,000. This gave us £1,460,000 as an income on which to base our expenditure. We have subsequently taken a similar cautious view because we have always started our budgetary preparations ahead of any declared figures from the DES. It is easier to add to expenditure but much more acrimonious to reduce it. There is also the psychological uplift of having a little extra to spend which puts the earlier sparring well into the background.

As we were using the Schools' Information Management System (SIMS), we decided to take their headings and to add our own sub-headings (see Table 5.1). We were aware that the sub-headings did not precisely accord with those in the pink section of the rainbow pack but we wanted the budget to have a day-to-day meaning in school rather than be designed solely to meet DES reporting requirements. In that first rough draft, everything was worked to the nearest £1,000 and anything less than that was ignored. Although we systematically allocated costs to each sub-heading as it occurred, the total expenditure figure was only £10,000 greater than our estimated income. We felt quite pleased with this and decided not to chance our good fortune further but to wait until a provisional figure was received.

This came through in February and showed that we had underestimated the income by more than the £10,000. We had the satisfaction of increasing our expenditure plans in a number of areas. It did not take long for the necessary adjustments to be made to balance budgeted expenditure against income and to have the figures available for the governors' consideration.

Trying to estimate the likely income can be almost as fraught as estimating

Table 5.1 Budget plan headings

STAFF COSTS Teaching staff NTS monthly NTS hourly Supply staff Peripatetic Other staff costs	**PREMISES OCCUPANCY** Water Fuel and electricity Cleaning materials Cleaning equipment maintenance Property insurance VAT
EDUCATION SUPPLIES Departmental funding	**SUPPLIES AND SERVICES** Meals subsidy Teachers' meals
PREMISES MAINTENANCE Building maintenance Grounds maintenance Outworks VAT	Special catering Staff fund Reprographics Telephones Admin. stationery Equipment maintenance
FURNITURE AND EQUIPMENT Office desks/chairs Teaching desks/chairs Kitchen equipment Other equipment VAT	Contents insurance NTA vacancy adverts Promotional activities Professional fees Bank charges VAT
EDUCATIONAL SERVICES Teaching equipment Exam fees	**BUDGETED EXPENDITURE**
Education visits subsidy Transport/travel Library service Teaching equipment maintenance Musical instruments TV licences Teacher vacancy adverts VAT	**INCOME** Catering Exam fees Lettings TVEI Interest AMG b/f from 1989–90
SPG SUPPORT In-service training	**BUDGETED INCOME**

expenditure. The AMG and TVEI figures were known and income from catering could be based on the previous year, but lettings was a different matter. The position with regard to the letting of the school premises changed when the school became grant-maintained. The LEA withdrew every adult education class which used the school, so a potential source of income was lost at a stroke. We had been fairly successful in attracting new lettings but could not guarantee this for the future. Similarly, income from bank deposits depends upon the amount on deposit and the interest rate and therefore cannot be predicted with any certainty. At the end of 1989 both were high but could change and plans to spend any surplus on the much needed physical improvements to the school could make the picture very different a year later.

Out of this came three guiding principles which have been used in the preparation or revision of subsequent budgets:

- Always assume there will be no carry-over from the previous year.
- Always overestimate the expenditure and underestimate the income.
- Always round up to the nearest thousand pounds.

VAT can be estimated easily because it is possible to identify those areas of expenditure which are subject to it. It is then necessary to multiply this total by the going rate to give the VAT figure for each main section. It is best to keep this separate because all invoices and most estimates separate it from the itemised costs.

The revision carried out in September 1990 (see Table 5.2) was done when our final AMG was increased by over £112,000 compared with the provisional figure. This allowed definite plans for a further financial injection into departments and a programme of classroom refurbishment to be realistic. As the year progressed, money was further vired against budget headings as actual costs became clearer and the Gulf War doubled the price of heating oil! Even so, our minds could not have been so befuddled that Christmas when we set the underlying budget because we made a trading surplus of £7,000 to add to the £88,000 carried forward from the previous year, which had been deliberately lost in the buildings maintenance budget.

Our budgeting process has changed radically with experience and now begins in the September of the previous financial year. Key members of staff who are responsible for substantial amounts of expenditure submit itemised bids for finance. Even the staffing salaries figure is submitted in this way before the bargaining begins about what may or may not be possible depending upon the likely AMG. At this point, the possibility of extending the standard scale or making enhanced payments between scales can be argued against the merits of appointing more teachers and giving everyone an extra non-teaching period. It is only in the heat of these discussions that the true cost of additional non-teaching periods becomes clear and whether or not staff covering for absent colleagues in order to save on supply costs is appropriate.

There is no doubt that opening up the debate on how money should be spent has brought about a greater awareness of the costs and diverse issues which affect a school. Importantly, greater involvement in the decision-making has brought about an appreciation and understanding of the problems. At school level the issues are more real and apparent and even disagreeable answers are more acceptable when the alternatives are understood. This does not mean that argument is muted, particularly when emotive issues like health and safety are used to drive home a point. In the end, there are certain costs which have to be met and it is the final tenth of the budget about which any real discussion can take place.

It is advisable not to make commitments for the future, simply to avoid

Table 5.2 Budget plan for financial year 1990–1

Category headings	Provisional (March)	Revised (September)
STAFF COSTS		
Teaching staff	910,600	930,000
NTS monthly	200,200	210,000
NTS hourly	44,100	50,000
Supply staff	15,100	30,000
Peripatetic	14,000	14,000
Other staff costs	16,000	6,000
Total	1,200,000	1,240,000
EDUCATION SUPPLIES		
Departmental funding	65,000	71,000
Total	65,000	71,000
PREMISES MAINTENANCE		
Building maintenance	47,325	140,000
Grounds maintenance	20,000	20,000
Outworks	5,000	5,000
VAT	8,250	20,000
Total	80,575	185,000
FURNITURE AND EQUIPMENT		
Office desks/chairs	1,000	1,000
Teaching desks/chairs	8,000	12,000
Kitchen equipment	1,000	1,000
Other equipment	2,500	3,000
VAT	1,875	3,000
Total	14,375	20,000
EDUCATIONAL SERVICES		
Teaching equipment	20,000	30,000
Exam fees	27,000	27,000
Education visits subsidy	5,000	5,000
Transport/travel	1,500	1,500
Library service	2,500	3,000
Teaching equipment maintenance	3,000	3,000
Musical instruments	2,000	2,000
TV licences	100	100
Teacher vacancy adverts	2,000	2,000
VAT	8,930	9,000
Total	72,030	82,600

continues . .

awkward discussion now. Much will happen in that intervening time to change the list of priorities. There is a need for a rolling programme so that next year means precisely that, even though the immediate concern is the current year. In this way, there is continual discussion about potentially major items of expenditure and an opportunity for the school to consider alternative ways of raising funds.

Table 5.2 Continued

Category headings	Provisional (March)	Revised (September)
SPG SUPPORT		
In-service training	13,000	13,000
Total	13,000	13,000
PREMISES OCCUPANCY		
Water	5,000	5,000
Fuel and electricity	28,000	42,000
Cleaning materials	3,000	4,000
Cleaning equipment maintenance	800	1,000
Property insurance	6,600	7,000
VAT	570	700
Subtotal	43,970	59,700
SUPPLIES AND SERVICES		
Meals' subsidy	16,000	19,713
Teachers' meals	0	4,000
Special catering	0	1,000
Staff fund	0	1,000
Reprographics	5,000	5,000
Telephones	7,000	7,000
Admin. stationery	1,000	1,000
Equipment maintenance	1,500	1.500
Contents insurance	11,000	11,000
NTA vacancy adverts	1,000	1,000
Promotional activities	3,000	10,000
Professional fees	12,000	11,000
Bank charges	0	1,000
VAT	3,675	4,000
Subtotal	61,175	78,213
BUDGETED EXPENDITURE	1,550,125	1,749,513
INCOME		
Catering	15,000	15,000
Exam fees	2,000	2,000
Lettings	7,000	7,000
TVEI	27,600	27,600
Interest	6,000	6,000
AMG	1,492,525	1,604,348
b/f from 1989–90	0	87,565
BUDGETED INCOME	1,550,125	1,749,513

Element two – specific bidding for discretionary funds

Capital grants

These come in two forms: named projects and a formula allocation. A system of bidding operates for named projects. Each year a financial circular letter is sent out to schools in July or August requesting information about capital projects for the following financial year. Priorities for capital allocation include:

- committed expenditure: projects begun before the school became grant-maintained but not completed until after incorporation or expenditure phased over a number of years where this is the second or subsequent year;
- major repair work such as work urgently needed to keep the premises in use;
- work required on health and safety grounds;
- work required to meet changes in education needs: in the first two years of capital bidding implementation of the National Curriculum.

The financial circular letter sets out how to apply and, to date, there has been very little guidance on the nature of the application. It is inadvisable to involve expensive professional advice at this stage except in the estimation of the cost of a scheme. It is important to cost schemes accurately as an overestimate could deprive another school of grant aid, while an underestimate could result in your school having to find the difference from other sources.

Assuming that the school's bid is successful, the real work then begins. The school will be bombarded with forms from the architects and buildings branch of the DES and these will oscillate backwards and forwards between the school and the DES until they are correct. At this stage it is appropriate to employ professional help in formalising the plans and completing some of the returns.

Grant allocated for a financial year is expected to be spent and claimed in that year. We met the invoices from our own funds for every agreed project and later claimed the money back. For much larger projects payment is usually phased and may be paid by the DES directly.

Whether the school is spending grant allocated for a named project or by formula, it is expected that a minimum of three tenders or quotes are obtained. The governors must have a declared tender policy which they rigidly apply. Approval will normally be given for the lowest figure unless there are compelling arguments why this should not be so. In such a case, it might be expected that the school finds the difference from its own resources. The arguments have to be equally compelling if three sets of figures are not submitted with the claim for approval. All of this takes time and, as major building work is usually reserved for the summer holidays, it is advisable to start the formal process as soon as the application for capital grant is approved. We learnt the hard way and had a refurbished technology area out of action because of a month's delay in completion. Firewalls and doors were built along corridors with students in session and we are about to replace windows one year after submitting the claim because we missed the only other opportunity during the summer holiday last year.

Special purpose grant: development

Each year in June, the DES publishes a draft circular inviting LEAs to apply for training grants. This circular outlines areas of training which are considered to be important in the forthcoming financial year. The government pays a 60 per cent grant to LEAs for training; the LEA provides the other 40 per cent. An allowance for this latter proportion of the expenditure is made in determining a grant-maintained school's AMG. In addition, grant-maintained schools are eligible for a special purpose grant, SPG(D), to cover training and development. At Queensbury we added £13,000 from AMG to the SPG(D) sum of, in round figures, £16,000, paid direct from the DES.

Again, it is necessary to bid for this grant using the criteria laid down in the appropriate financial circular letter. For the financial year 1990–91, at least one-third had to be spent on subjects related to the basic curriculum, at least one-third had to be spent on GEST-related activities and not more than one-third on local priorities.

Special purpose grant: restructuring

SPG(R) is a one-off payment for newly incorporated grant-maintained schools. It provides governors with the opportunity to restructure the teaching staff during the first year after achieving the status. The governors may feel that certain decisions involving redundancy, early retirement or voluntary severance are necessary in the interests of the efficient operation of the school. Any claim is subject to the approval of the Secretary of State and has to be implemented within two years of incorporation.

Special purpose grant: VAT

SPG(V) is designed to help compensate grant-maintained schools for some of the cost of VAT which they are not able to reclaim. The remaining VAT charges that they are required to pay are balanced against the rate relief that grant-maintained schools get in respect of their charitable status. These figures may not balance out. The grant is paid at the rate of 2.5 per cent of AMG less the amount of any reduced rate liability. This grant is paid automatically and if the relief from rates liability is greater than the amount paid in VAT there is no requirement to pay back the excess to the DES.

THE INTERNAL AUDIT

To emphasise the seriousness which the DES place on the guidance given in the rainbow pack, each grant-maintained school is subject to inspection by the internal audit division (IAD) of the DES. Our experience was that they visited the school after we had opened as a grant-maintained school although, as it turned out, the advice they offered would have been more useful before incorporation. The purpose of the visit, which can last for several days, is to inspect the financial control systems to ensure that the public money is being properly used and appropriate accounting systems are in place. Sadly, we got a well-deserved 'hammering' in our first IAD report, the basis of which could be traced to our ill-defined bursarial appointment. It was clear from the report that necessary controls were lacking and urgent remedies were necessary. The governors were stung into action.

THE ANNUAL ACCOUNTS

All accounts held by the school, including the school fund, have to be opened to scrutiny by the auditors. The choice of auditor is for the governors to decide. It is important that the firm has no links with the school because independence at this level is paramount. The governors may choose a local or national firm. At Queensbury we arranged to interview a number of firms of different sizes to learn of their experience at this level of accounting, what educational involvement they might have had and what additional services they might offer. In our short-listing we eliminated small firms that did not have any medium-sized business experience and included those with an educational background.

Like all professional services, the school will pay for what it gets so it is important to obtain a list of their charges. If the contract is purely for auditing purposes, the assessment of the interviewees will be based on different criteria from those appropriate to other financial services. We found that a national firm with a local branch came out best on the basic audit and the additional service costs. A secondary school could expect to pay about £5,000 for the audit and preparation of accounts.

The auditor spends about two weeks in the school analysing the books and allocating income and expenditure to the correct heading. The annual financial return is prepared by a different branch of the firm so that the audit is still independent of all other scrutiny.

Once the auditor has prepared draft accounts, they are sent to the school together with a draft of the proposed management letter. The management letter will make reference to accounting practices within the school which the auditor feels should change because they are unsatisfactory. A response will be invited to the accounts and the management letter, and schools are well advised to respond. These documents form the basis of the formal audit report which is sent to the DES. The fact that the school has responded is noted in the final draft. Not surprisingly, Queensbury had a bad audit report for the first year, but for the second year showed a vast improvement.

The audited accounts are presented to the governing body before they are sent to the DES. This enables the governors to question all aspects of the accounts, including the management letter. This is really the last opportunity to influence what is sent to the DES. Although governors do question the content of the report, it is usually to query points that they do not fully understand rather than to challenge the report. Following a resolution of the governors to accept the audit report, a bond copy is signed by the chairman and the auditor and sent to the DES.

At the end of the first financial year, the transitional grant account will also be audited. Unlike the AMG, the school has had to submit a bid for the transitional grant. The auditors will assess the bid against the actual expenditure and, while it is almost impossible to spend exactly the amount forecast in the bid, a check will be made that all expenditure is within the allowable categories. Any grant not spent in the appropriate way will be recovered by the DES from the following year's AMG, together with any underspending of the grant.

COMPUTERISED ACCOUNTING SYSTEMS

The need for financial information is considerable in a grant-maintained school. Financial decisions can only be based on readily accessible and accurate financial information, preferably stored in computer files.

A school needs to consider what it wants from its accounting system and how that financial information is to be presented. Two software packages, SIMS and AIMS, have financial modules which will produce the information for the DES returns. However, they are not accounts packages and, if the school is also running its own payroll, there is need of an accounts package which can be adapted to give the DES information. At Queensbury we chose the latter option because we run one of the recognised payroll packages which can be supplemented by its own accounts package. At the time of writing we are in the process of making the transition from a manual to a computerised system because of the difficulty in getting information rapidly from the manual system. It is advisable to run both systems in parallel before using the computer system exclusively. We are manually recording information as well until we are fully confident and competent with the software. In due course we will extend to computer order processing and cheque writing so that all financial transactions are computer-based.

It is worth making a special mention of a payroll facility. As a prospective grant-maintained school we were bombarded by payroll companies wanting to run our payroll for us. My advice is to contract out to an LEA prepared to offer this facility at a competitive price because LEAs specialise in payrolls for educational establishments. As one of the first grant-maintained schools we did not have the benefit of this; LEAs had not considered selling their services at the time. We had no choice but to consider using a payroll agency or doing it ourselves. When it became clear what was expected of schools even when payrolling had been contracted to an agency we quickly realised that, with only a little extra effort, we could run it ourselves. It is not difficult for a school to run its own payroll once it has set up a nationally-recognised payroll programme.

For all systems, there is a need for manual controls and checks. These controls should be applied to all aspects of a computerised system so that errors can be quickly identified. Operator error is usually the cause of mistakes and, as long as this is accepted and the necessary controls are in force, the computer will save both time and staffing costs in an area of operations which can be very complex.

OVERALL IMPRESSIONS

After two years we are looking forward to the third. Certainly it has been very hard work and there have been mistakes. Early errors are still being rectified and the problems arising from the ill-defined bursarial post have only recently disappeared. Nevertheless one has to take an overview and acknowledge that the opportunity to plan everything for the school has been exciting and there is great satisfaction in using the financial freedom to enable the school to provide the education that it believes is appropriate for its intake. The bottom line must be 'does the student benefit?'. It is this ability to influence educational change that is so rewarding. Importantly, through grant-maintained status, a school can respond positively to its needs and can realistically plan in discussions involving all colleagues so that everyone is part of the process. Discussion can also be widened to include parents, students and whoever else needs to be involved. The word I use frequently is 'ownership'. Everyone has a shared interest and a part to play because success depends upon all and not just a few. Commitment can be expressed in a genuine way. The head is no longer merely keeping the ship afloat, but involved in stoking the boilers and plotting a course with sustained educational improvement as its destination.

Chapter 6

Managing capital development
Contracts and premises

Brother Francis, Headteacher at St Francis Xavier College in Liverpool describes the approach his school has adopted over the past two years to the management of contracts and premises.

The headteacher and governors were fortunate in having some relevant experience as both a direct grant and voluntary-aided school prior to grant-maintained status and have been able to build on this in their management of contracts and premises more recently. The school was incorporated in September 1989.

INTRODUCTION

Approval for grant-maintained status signals the responsibility for buildings and premises being transferred to the governors along with all other responsibilities. In the intervening time before incorporation as a grant-maintained school, the governors are partners with the LEA in determining any alterations to premises and plant. No alterations to the buildings should be pursued without the authorisation of the governors. All assets within the buildings transfer to the governors at incorporation and may not be removed by the LEA without governor approval. It is perhaps a time when the ultimate responsibilities of the governing body in relation to their new self-governing role are fine-tuned and understood. The responsibilities for the whole school environment become a priority.

St Francis Xavier's College was a direct grant grammar school up to 1983 and as such was responsible for all buildings. The architect who built the school in 1960 continued his interest and involvement under direct grant regulations. From 1983 to 1990, as a voluntary-aided school, the trustees had certain responsibilities for the external maintenance while the LEA should have looked after the interior decoration and maintenance. We have been fortunate to have had previous experience in direct responsibility for maintenance and to have had the services of an architect direct. To take on this responsibility again, but as a grant-maintained school was both welcome and challenging. A county school will have had less experience than a voluntary-aided school in the direct management of building maintenance.

The Educational Assets Board will prepare for the transfer of the property deeds and determine the extent of assets to be transferred to the governors. This takes a considerable burden away from the new grant-maintained school. During the inevitable delay in finalising assets the governors must take the buildings 'as seen' and assess the condition of the whole.

MANAGING PREMISES

Here at St Francis Xavier's College the building and development committee of the governors was given delegated powers to take decisions regarding immediate as well as long-term planning for building and maintenance. A small contractor advised this committee on the state of buildings at incorporation and continues to do so at six-monthly intervals. A programme of refurbishment followed from this advice for the first year of operation. The governors took a very basic decision at the beginning of our life as a grant-maintained school – that any immediate benefits arising from becoming grant-maintained must be felt in the classroom. Complete redecoration of the interior of both school sites was seen as important for providing a pleasant educational environment. A phased programme is nearing completion. Any structural advice was referred to the architect. Health and safety aspects took priority in any maintenance work. An observant caretaker linked these agents for improvement and proved to be a strong line of communication with the headteacher. It must become obvious that considerable additional work results from the new responsibilities. The tremendous advantage of being able to fund such improvements without delay from a budget set by the finance committee is ample reward for the extra work. Actually seeing improvements take place on a large scale is a boost to the morale of staff and to the interest of the students.

Managing premises with a planned programme can be funded only from the annual maintenance grant (AMG). Most schools will similarly have a long list of needs and an inability to satisfy immediately all demands for improvement. We are now in our third financial year and the unfolding pattern of maintenance is now very visible thanks to a third allocation from the AMG. This year we are concentrating on renewing classroom furniture and equipment, again with the intention of improving the whole school environment: seventeen classrooms will be completely refurnished in this programme.

Arranging contracts for such maintenance gives the governors a greater degree of control over standards of work and deadlines. It is important to arrange contracts with a heating engineer, electrical engineers, glazing contractors, plumbing contractors and the like so that at very short notice emergencies can be dealt with. We have found it possible to have a contractor on site within an hour for an emergency or broken window – such is the power of holding the purse strings.

We have two swimming pools, one on each site. The daily maintenance is important and requires a certain expertise from qualified personnel. Our governors decided to buy in the services of the LEA for the first year under the contract conditions set by the LEA with their direct works programme. Although the governors found the LEA expensive they needed time to look at alternative contractors or take on an employee with the appropriate technical skills. A swimming pool is a sensitive area where regulations are concerned and our governors decided that they could not be too careful.

Energy conservation is very much to the fore at present and there is no shortage of companies offering consultation, expertise and advice for a percentage of the savings. We have had surveys on water saving, electrical energy saving by moving away from tungsten to strip lighting, gas energy saving on central heating as well as insulation advice generally. The governors have taken the results of surveys into account in the management of premises and the maintenance work they have approved. Our two swimming pools will be under the microscope this year for possible energy conservation since they are proving to be very expensive to run.

CAPITAL BIDDING AND CONTRACTS

Each financial year a grant-maintained school is invited to bid for capital funding. It is important to prepare such a bid carefully and in good time to meet deadlines. One of the difficult tasks for governors and their advisers is to pitch their bid so that it is 'in tune' with the priorities and thinking of the DES. Furthermore, it is important that the scope of work planned can be seen through within a financial year. It is more difficult to convince the DES on a rolling programme spanning a number of years, even though the governors would wish to plan long term.

In our situation, before grant-maintained status was contemplated, the LEA had earmarked St Francis Xavier's to be developed as a single-site school from its two sites two miles apart. As a voluntary-aided school such single-site development had been favourably considered by the DES. In 1983 there were talks taking place to promote the school towards the 'design list' stage which, once reached, guarantees a capital programme.

Our first bid for capital funding was based on a total development over five years. The governors costed each phase and submitted a bid for the first year but without success. The DES did finance from capital grant heavy-duty equipment for the new design and technology accommodation up to £80,000 and agreed that all asbestos be removed, up to a cost of £90,000 maximum. This was work that became outstanding from the time we were under the LEA.

The whole process of submitting a capital bid requires the professional services of an architect and quantity surveyor since the attention to detail required in the DES forms, known as ABB forms (architect and buildings), demands more expertise than is to be found within a school. Such forms go up as far as ABB12 before final financial settlement for a project is reached so it is apparent that a measure of bureaucracy still exists outside the LEA! Completion of such forms depends on good communication and co-operation from the many interested parties within the school. All such input has an important bearing on the final building project submitted, since it will incorporate more ideas from those who will use the new provision.

With hindsight our particular bid was too general in that it was titled 'Phase 1 of 5 to Follow' although the costings were accurate, the project was discrete and represented a realistic figure of what could be spent in one year. It did however commit the DES to a rolling programme of capital funding over the next five years: an ambitious desire some might say especially with a general election due.

The other aspect of the capital grant is the formula allocation to each school based on numbers of pupils. This allocation is given on an annual basis and the amount is fixed by the DES and given in writing to each grant-maintained school. There is no blanket approval for spending such allocation. Each school submits a capital improvements scheme for DES approval and funding is forthcoming following such approval. ABB forms are used to go through the stages of estimate, tendering and contracting. Our first allocation was spent to give accommodation to provide for a bursar and her assistant. Since our incorporation date was 1 January 1990 our capital formula allocation was for three months only. This was sufficient to go beyond the planning stage and covered architect's fees and other professional outgoings. Final approval came from the DES in the next financial year 1990–91 and the new capital formula allocation saw the project through and the extension is now in full use. In the current financial year our allocation will be used for walk-in storage rooms within each of seventeen classrooms. The demands for storage space in each classroom made by the National Curriculum will now be met.

We have not so far succeeded in making any progress, in terms of bricks and mortar, towards a single-site school. It is even possible that we are further behind where we might have been had we remained a voluntary-aided school – not that this conjecture puts any blight on the decision we made to seek grant-maintained status. Our time will surely come.

When the good news announcing grant-maintained status is received by a school it is time to look at those areas under LEA responsibility that will come under the direct management of the governors. The obvious areas that spring to mind include staff contracts, catering, cleaning and grounds maintenance.

On incorporation day all staff pass to the employment of the governors with existing contracts and conditions of employment protected. The governors must agree to honour such previous conditions as salary and wage levels. Teaching staff continue with their existing contracts if they have not taken steps three months previously to seek alternative employment with the LEA or elsewhere. Their position is relatively straightforward and no new written contract of employment will be necessary.

Catering staff will transfer to the school with the governors as employers if the governors decide to offer an in-house catering service. This basic decision will depend on the relationships that existed between the LEA, the catering staff and the school prior to opting out. It may further depend on the standard of catering facilities that already exist. Among the schools that took an early route to grant-maintained status some chose in-house, but many decided to go for contract catering from one of the experienced school contract catering companies. St Francis Xavier's chose the latter route because of the desire to move away from the regeneration of frozen foods to fresh food catering. Two aspects were immediately evident in such a decision. A contract would involve personnel as well as a level of service. Our governors made a basic decision to include a pre-tender condition for any catering service that a contract caterer might offer. It was a condition of tender that all existing personnel who wished to stay at the school in a catering capacity were to be offered employment by the successful caterers. This ensured that the governors would not become involved in any possible redundancy claims since continuity of employment would be guaranteed. It had the added advantage of starting with a team who were familiar with the school and its catering. In the event some did choose to stay with the LEA who offered employment while others were willing to transfer employment to the successful tenderer.

Other reasons prevailed upon the governors in reaching this decision. They were aware of the increasing demands being made on establishments regarding standards of hygiene and the regulations relating to catering in particular. The whole area of the nutritional value of foods, balanced diets and variety demanded an expertise as well as qualifications. Health and safety regulations applicable to catering establishments were also part of the picture. Who in the school community possessed the necessary expertise? I was the first to register a disclaimer to such talents. Since the necessary skills had to be brought in, the professional caterer appeared to be the answer. In our case there was an additional reason for this decision. When we had been a direct grant school, catering was a school responsibility and we had received an excellent service in that period of self-government. In fact permission was sought and granted for us to return to our former catering company. They were happy to tender and our professional relationship started up again. I recognise that each school will have particular circumstances that will recommend themselves to governors and thus point to a catering decision. In the end the performance indicator is the take-up rate of meals by the customers: the pupils. We have found a daily increase from 220 per day under the LEA to 780 per day under our contract caterer. This has resulted in an easier lunch hour for the few teaching staff involved and more children remaining on site.

The cleaning contract will also revolve around the welfare of personnel. Existing staff must be satisfied that their employment is secure, possibly by direct employment by the governors under the direction of the caretaker. This has proved to be a popular route. Our catering contractor was also offering a housekeeping service and we negotiated the transfer of existing staff to the same company and a school cleaning contract was agreed. Many of the catering staff became housekeeping staff after their catering duties were over. In this way we were able to give full-time rather than part-time work. An additional feature has emerged. Catering and cleaning staff feel as strong a loyalty to the school as to their company, and both company and their staff have developed a strong loyalty to the school.

Our solution to catering and cleaning facilities has resulted in the only joint catering/cleaning contract I know of in the grant-maintained sector. Some of the advantages include a single management fee for both services and easy control of finances since a monthly invoice covers both staff and service costs with a clear printout giving ample detail. All ordering for catering needs and cleaning supplies and materials is part of their management responsibility and this considerably diminishes the paperwork in the bursar's office. The company offer in-service training to both catering and housekeeping staff as part of the service and our staff from catering and cleaning are always ready to oblige on special occasions. We are very satisfied with both services under a single contractor based on two contracts that run on an annual basis.

The contract for ground maintenance will vary even more from school to school depending on the extent of external premises. A school without playing fields will be a different challenge from a school with a large estate attached. The one will require a gardener whilst the larger will gladly use the expertise of perhaps several groundsmen to keep all in good order. A combination of both is not beyond possibility. The Education Assets Board will determine the extent of the premises, including playing fields, but maintenance contracts will be required before it finally produces a deed of transfer to the governing body.

A number of schools have been happy to buy in the services of their LEA for ground maintenance. Our position is unusual. We have twenty-four acres with substantial playing fields. In our former direct grant days, because we had total responsibility for the premises, we had both staff and equipment to fulfil such responsibility. During the six years under the LEA we lost the exclusive employment of our two full-time staff and under the LEA time-and-motion-exercise our entitlement became one person for three and a half days per week. It became normal to wave to one of them cutting grass verges and the centre of roundabouts while we were in transit between sites. The deterioration of our grounds was such that I enjoyed many a Saturday afternoon myself pulling gang mowers with a 'David Brown' (much to the chagrin of a certain trade union!). Although we had lost the exclusive services of our two groundsmen we had kept all our equipment and this was still in place when grant-maintained status was granted. We therefore found ourselves all geared up to bring the grounds back up to the level of maintenance to which we were accustomed. Our two groundsmen returned to the employment of the governors. There is now a generous budget to ensure they have job satisfaction and security. Our governors are happy that the grounds are pleasant to live in and the cricket square is hard with an even bounce!

A minor contract that might be easily overlooked is the annual maintenance and inspection of the gymnasium, its fixtures and movable equipment. We are fortunate in having a specialist company to hand in the locality and they are engaged to produce a defects report and a maintenance programme resulting therefrom. Similar contracts for heavy equipment and catering appliance maintenance will be drawn up as a matter of urgency, for reasons of safety.

A most important contract which has a vital bearing on personnel, buildings and contents as well as activities is the insurance contract. Many openings exist ranging from brokers who specialise in school insurances to companies who insure whole authorities or individual schools and the market is competitive. We chose the brokerage route and our package includes personnel aspects from employer's liability to staff travel and effects and pupil accident, and, on the material side, buildings and contents, public liability, theft and 'all risks' right down to breakages and losses. At the end of the day the governors must be confident that they have sound insurance cover arranged in packages so that the number of policies is kept to a minimum, premiums are competitive and commensurate with the cover offered and backed up by a thoroughly professional service.

We have found contact with the Health and Safety Executive a useful support in setting up appropriate procedures to ensure safe premises and contents. Their publications on health and safety at work and codes of practice will be of great assistance in formulating the school's specific health and safety policy. This policy document will be an important tool in the management of buildings and grounds and for in-service training to all who have a role to play in the maintenance programme of buildings and premises.

The contracts referred to are not in any way exhaustive. The whole area of leasing contracts opens up a very wide field. We have limited such contracts to reprographic equipment and now communications. Each school must assess its own needs and decide on outright purchase against a leasing policy. Whichever course is taken there are management implications for resources whether for curriculum or general need.

The Environmental Protection Act 1990 gives specific attention to school premises. There is now considerable awareness within the school of environmental issues and their importance. The code of practice on litter and refuse has implications on the management of premises to achieve Grade A, which must be regarded as the norm. The benefits of this is pupil involvement in the awareness of their school environment and their responsibilities in maintaining and improving matters. Ultimately their respect for buildings and surroundings will carry them into their own local community better equipped to be positive contributors and welcome young citizens.

In all this the reader might be questioning demarcation responsibilities within the governing body and the senior management team of the school.

Basically, at St Francis Xavier's College the governors agree policy across a wide spectrum of important issues and senior management implement and manage. This gives considerable responsibility to senior management but we feel it is the only way forward. Governors do not have offices within the school and the time between meetings of governors is such that important decisions must be made in the interim. We make an important distinction between governing and managing, and management decisions are taken without involving governors immediately; they become *au fait* at appropriate meetings. We do have an executive committee of three governors who consult over important decisions that need to be made between meetings of the full board. In this way life can go on with just a termly meeting of the full board of governors following a cycle of meetings of the four committees within the governing body.

Chapter 7

Managing the school
The role of governors and staff management structures

Professor Ray Page, Chairman of Governors at Bullers Wood School for Girls discusses some of the significant changes for a governing body when a school becomes grant-maintained. He had been connected with the school for thirteen years before it achieved grant-maintained status, as parent, governor, LEA adviser and senior officer. Throughout the chapter there is an emphasis on the differing roles of the governing body and the school's senior management team. Bullers Wood School was incorporated as grant-maintained on 1 January 1991.

INTRODUCTION

Governors of grant-maintained schools, like the headteachers of these schools, face a considerable change in their role and function when their school gains this status. As one colleague governor, who is also a governor of a county LEA-maintained school commented to me recently:

> I have to think and take on real responsibilities when I attend meetings here as well as becoming involved in the life of the school other than just at its special functions. On the other governing body I attend, I sit for three hours once a term and am expected to endorse what the LEA wants to do even though it does not appear to be in the best interests of the school. I only attend school events when asked.

The change is less dramatic for governors of voluntary-aided schools and those schools that have been piloting LMS. While the additional duties may appear to be daunting, this does not seem to have dissuaded existing governors from continuing to serve, and as yet, there have been no difficulties in filling vacancies. The pattern could change and the DES is concerned that governor recruitment may be more difficult when the four-year 'peak' of appointments comes up for renewal in 1992. However, the comment above is typical of many I have heard and, given the real job to do and community involvement, backed up by effective governor training, we can be optimistic about future recruitment and commitment to the governance of grant-maintained schools.

As the governing bodies are drawn from parents, teachers and people connected with the local community, including commerce and industry, they tend to have more direct impact upon, and expect feedback from, the delivery of the curriculum in terms of relevance and effectiveness, getting value for money, and links with the community. It has, therefore, come as a surprise to some schools, our own included, that the opposition to grant-maintained status has been so strong, particularly as such status may be regarded as the culmination of LMS. Dealing with this opposition is frequently the first change in their role that the newly formed governing body face; namely, being very much more in the public eye and having to 'keep your head when all around are losing theirs'. For many governors this is the first taste of marketing and public relations and can be daunting especially as the market can contain hostile elements.

MARKETING AND PUBLIC RELATIONS

Irrespective of its political balance, an LEA has little to gain and much to lose if it no longer has control of a school. Its own admissions procedure will be more difficult to operate as well as it losing part of the funds that pay for central services so that these services may have to be reduced. Additionally the LEA loses a capital asset although it has to continue to pay any debt charges outstanding at the time of transfer. This may explain why LEA opposition has transcended political affiliation in so many cases.

On top of this, grant-maintained schools have been able to take on their additional responsibilities in terms of contracting services and managing finance, sites and buildings and the personnel function in a relatively short space of time, such that this challenges the pace, complexity and amount of devolution with which LEAs are introducing LMS. Thus members and officers are likely to offer fierce opposition to grant-maintained status which in turn may lead to an overstatement on their part in response to the reasons given by the governors for wishing to opt out.

Previously, few governors have had to face parents other than at speech day or the annual parents' meeting, let alone speak to an apologia and answer questions in a context that can be hostile. Indeed the LEA governor representatives may themselves actively oppose the move so that there is internal tension to face as well.

In our case, opting out did not arise from a closure threat or such reasons as the school wishing to remain or become a selective school. It was already a successful girls' all-ability school with applications exceeding places by three to one, good examination results, particularly with respect to average pupils, and an established reputation for science and technology. Additionally there had already been a positive vote by the governors against opting out when this first became an option, although this alternative was reconsidered when the LEA, in response to the Greenwich judgement, decided to halt the then current catchment area admissions policy and replace it with a zoning policy which they felt complied with the law.

Its immediate impact on our school was to reduce applications to two to one because of the risk parents had to take to apply to a school outside their zone and our zone was made up largely of a cemetery and a golf course! In addition, although the local inspectorate had praised the quality of the science and technology teaching they had condemned the out-of-date accommodation.

The governors passed the first resolution in the hope that the consultation with the LEA would bring some agreement to review the admission policy and give a higher priority to the refurbishment of the laboratories. When a negative response was received from the LEA the parents took the matter out of the governors' hands by presenting a petition and, after the appropriate consultation, forced a second ballot.

Our stance was to be reasonable and to try to avoid confrontation with the LEA. To do this we had three public meetings. At the first meeting the governors who were committed to grant-maintained status each dealt with one aspect of it or gave their reasons for supporting it. At the end of the meeting the chairman provided an overview of the reasons for seeking the status and invited questions. At the next meeting the LEA presented its case against the school's proposal to go grant-maintained and the headteacher of an established grant-maintained school spoke about the advantages of opting out. The governors listened to the debate and thereby avoided being drawn in to making unconsidered replies which could have allowed the LEA to fuel any dispute between governors, as amateurs, and LEA officers, as professionals. The final meeting consisted mainly of questions and answers with the LEA representative governor opposed to the move involved in the debate. This was a very difficult meeting and with hindsight we should have engaged an independent chairperson, but by countering the LEA's claims about the impact on the school of opting out both at these meetings and by issuing bulletins, the process of consultation remained reasonably dignified. The ballot was an overwhelming yes.

Previously, governors had only been required to make representation to the LEA, and had not had to defend their decision so publicly in the context of the local press misrepresenting the issues and trying to get an inside story. This experience welded the governing body into a team more quickly than any other team-building activity could have done and this made the transitional period very much easier to negotiate as well as the subsequent functioning of the governing body after incorporation.

MANAGEMENT STYLE AND RELATIONS WITH STAFF

Stating that the governors are responsible for policy and the headteacher for the day-to-day running of the school is an oversimplification of the complexity of the relationship between the governors and staff, and in particular the chairman and headteacher. To draw the analogy of a company board of directors to the senior management, and the chairman and managing director or chief executive, where these posts are separated, may help the understanding of some governors who have had experience of such companies, but is not really helpful to those that have not. To begin to understand the complexity of the situation let me quote the grant-maintained governors' guide on curriculum responsibilities:

In brief the governors:

- provide the headteacher with a copy of the up-to-date statement of their policy on the curriculum;
- ensure that the school provides the National Curriculum and carries out other curriculum duties;
- ensure that the school offers only qualifications or syllabuses approved by the Secretary of State;
- ensure the school provides religious education and daily collective worship;
- establish a complaints procedure;
- ensure that the school provides information which they are required to provide to parents and others.

The headteacher:

- is responsible for day-to-day decisions about the management and curriculum of the school in line with the governors' statement on the curriculum;
- can decide that the National Curriculum shall not apply, or shall apply differently, to an individual pupil for a temporary period;
- carries out the duties as outlined in the governors' curriculum statement.

Generally, governors will not be able to draw up a curriculum statement without the help and advice of the headteacher, unless they bring in outside expertise. As the framework of much of the curriculum is defined by the National Curriculum, 'buying in' outside expertise to ascertain the reasonableness and acceptability of the headteacher's proposals is not normally necessary. However, the broad balance of the curriculum and its emphasis should be decided by the governors within the context of their knowledge of the community and the aspirations of parents. For example, they may feel that not sufficient attention is given to the creative arts or indeed the opposite. Their role, as defined by law, demands this much, but it should not go further to start defining the way a particular course should be taught. That is for the professional staff to determine. In other words, the community which a grant-maintained school serves should have a say through the governing body in what constitutes the curriculum (bearing in mind that teachers are represented on the governing body), but the delivery of the curriculum should be in the hands of the headteacher and the teaching staff.

It is not easy for governors to keep the balance between formulating policy and interfering in the day-to-day running of the school, without being criticised for lack of commitment and involvement. There are several strategies for avoiding this difficulty.

First, if governors are all involved in the formulation of policy and decisions affecting the long-term future of the school, they are less likely to want to get involved in the day-to-day running of the school. At Bullers Wood we have set up a number of sub-committees to deal with our statutory obligations (admissions, appeals, pupil discipline) and other important areas (finance and general purposes, staffing, the French centre) and to advise the full governing body about matters in these areas. This means that the full governing body only has to meet twice a term for two to three hours, and every governor is involved in at least one sub-committee whose membership never exceeds seven. These are effectively task groups in which even the most reticent governor feels able to take part and contribute. Indeed, some schools have set up specific task groups to achieve the same result rather than sub-committees. We do not have a curriculum committee as such, but task groups are constituted in this area when needed.

Second, if governors are attached to a year group and subject area, and are invited into school on a regular basis by staff with responsibilities in these areas they gain an insight into the day-to-day work of the school without intrusion or disruption.

Third, a school can organise an open day for governors where they can tour the school in small groups and join in activities to get a flavour of the work going on. As long as such events are handled sensitively, most teachers are more than willing to contribute to the marketing of their school. There are many variations on this theme, such as a governor with a particular interest in mathematics spending a half day in that department, which may have the added bonus of establishing a school–industry link when the governor has appropriate connections in the community.

In this new role of policy maker there are two other dangers for the governing body. One danger is that they will be criticised by the staff and parents for being too remote and for a lack of perception in the same way that the LEA was previously blamed. The attachment strategy described above, and to some extent the task group approach, particularly where senior staff are involved in groups with governors, are some strategies that help to allay these fears. However, to a certain extent these approaches can encourage the second danger – that of staff trying to involve governors in an issue when they do not agree with the headteacher's decision. Individual governors should not become involved in such disputes because they do not have the authority to act as an individual but only as part of a corporate body. Governing bodies need to take care that they only become involved if, in their opinion, a headteacher fails to resolve an issue satisfactorily.

In this context, the unions may try to obtain signed recognition agreements from the governing body which would mean that disciplinary and grievance procedures would have to be negotiated rather than be determined by the governing body after consulting the staff. Again this is likely to be a new area for consideration by both governors and senior staff and it is worth bearing in mind that the model articles of government for grant-maintained schools only require the governing body to consult with staff in such circumstances. At Bullers Wood, the governors have resisted direct consultation with the unions and delegated the responsibility to the headteacher who holds regular meetings with all the union representatives.

The annual parents' meeting is one event at which the governors are able to discharge their responsibilities to the parents of the pupils in the school, although another approach to this is to send regular newsletters to the parents through their children. We are carefully monitoring the complaints that have been received, but are also being more proactive by sending a questionnaire to parents about all the school's activities and issues that are likely to be of concern to the parents. This includes questions on curriculum provision, resources, school meals and the state of the buildings.

As yet we have not attempted any joint governor–staff training to build up stronger relationships between governors and staff, although three heads of study (in Mathematics, English, Science and Technology) have made presentations to governors during a one-day training session that we held for governors. It is likely that the first joint training will take place at the time of the first annual review of our embryonic business plan.

SCHOOL BUSINESS PLANS

When a school has moved through the transition phase, and the period immediately following incorporation, the senior management and governors of a school are probably sufficiently well known to one another and the governors sufficiently familiar with the work of the school for the two groups to work together to produce a business plan. Even with the advent of LMS, there has been a tendency for school development plans to accentuate curriculum planning and then confine themselves to the staffing and resourcing of particular curriculum initiatives, so that staff development, accommodation, finance and management issues only relate to specific items. This means that an analysis of strengths and weakness, opportunities and threats on a broader basis is frequently overlooked.

Management structures need to be examined in the light of the overall changes that are required including marketing the school and recruitment of staff and pupils. The plan must take into account the curriculum and staff development requirements and involve appropriate capital development that is not viewed solely in terms of maintenance of the site and buildings as they currently exist, but in terms of its suitability for the curriculum being (and to be) delivered. In other words, a more balanced and outward plan is required which illuminates the differences in the roles of governors and the senior staff. For grant-maintained schools a business plan needs to combine all these aspects because the LEA is no longer there to look after any of the external aspects which traditionally it has dealt with. I appreciate that this is something of an oversimplification and that for some years many LEAs have been working towards effective partnership, with their schools taking on much more responsibility for the external matters than perhaps my remarks suggest.

A business plan of the kind I have indicated can only be effectively devised and put into effect when the governors and senior management in a school are working closely together. Hence my earlier comment that some time needs to elapse after incorporation before such a venture should be attempted. Even then there must be a high level of trust, confidence and freedom from any patronising attitudes by both groups. As suggested earlier, the team spirit frequently developed during the period up to the submission of a proposal to the Secretary of State and during the transitional phase can go a long way to produce this kind of relationship. So too can joint training events.

Some governing bodies and senior management teams have developed their plans by agreeing headings and then spending some time together free from interruption developing these headings and setting up task groups to write particular sections. Some schools have supported this process by providing residential accommodation for governors and senior staff over a weekend period while others have involved an educational consultancy to act as honest broker. Some have used both strategies.

To date we have not used either of these approaches although we may do so when we revise and refine our document. Our initial plan was produced by the headteacher and myself agreeing the headings that needed to be developed and taking account of the existing school development plan produced under the aegis of the LEA. Various sections were then drafted by the senior management team involving governors as appropriate. The governing body as a whole then considered, altered and approved the final draft so that the final plan was strategic in its terms. The senior management team then developed an internal plan for discussion with the whole staff which was operational in its terms, setting particular goals with respect to curriculum delivery, resource management, planned maintenance and refurbishment, and so on.

There is no definitive set of headings that can be identified for school business plans. We used the following:

Brief outline of the school's background.
Mission statement giving the school's overall aims.
Financial organisation and income generation.
Curriculum delivery and resource management.
Recruitment and marketing.
The administration.
Quality assurance and staff development.

GOVERNOR TRAINING

The last section mentioned joint staff and governor training, and this seems, therefore, a good point to comment on governor training generally. It is a difficult topic on the following counts:

- Who appraises the governors' training needs, bearing in mind what is wanted is not the same as what is needed? (I may need to go to the dentist, but I will not necessarily want to go)
- Should the training be internally or externally organised? (For example, should a head of department brief governors on her or his subject with respect to the National Curriculum or should outside educational advisers do this training?)
- Given the time governors already give on a voluntary basis, how much more time can they be expected to spend on training?

If not properly organised, joint governor and staff training may lead to a worsening of relationships rather than their improvement and factions begin to appear that can interfere both in the day-to-day running of the school or the long-term planning.

Evidence to date suggests that these difficulties can be overcome and governors can be very positive about such training. With respect to the first point above, an outside consultant can help by acting as an honest broker, and there is no reason why the second item cannot be carefully blended to provide a balance of both with heads of department giving the occasional presentation before a governor's meeting by way of an introduction. If governors can acquire an understanding of the educational system and their role as governors within it through such training, less time will be spent during meetings trying to tease out such matters. However, joint training should only be undertaken when both sides feel this will be mutually beneficial. It is also important for the headteacher and chairman of governors to have a strong working relationship which recognises the pressures that each face. For example, unless retired, many chairpersons will be in full-time employment and this will place strictures on their availability and time. Arranging governor meetings at the beginning of the new school year may give the headteacher insufficient time to prepare the necessary reports and produce an overload at a very important time in the school calendar.

ADMISSIONS AND COMPLAINTS

In the grant-maintained context the governors will have determined the admissions policy as part of their proposal to the Secretary of State, which he will either have accepted or requested to be modified in granting approval. The governors will then be responsible for implementing this policy without fear or favour, including setting up an appeals mechanism. This will be a new activity for most governors and for those sitting on any appeals panel some training is likely to be necessary to ensure consistency of approach. Independent chairpersons will also have to be found as well as a clerk for each panel. Because we expected a high number of appeals with over 400 applications for 170 places, we constituted an admissions sub-committee of three – the chairman, the vice-chairman and the headteacher – leaving the remaining twelve governors (excluding the two teacher governors) free to service the three appeal panels that were set up. In this way we were able to clear all the appeals in two Saturday sittings. We also asked one governor to monitor the operation of the three panels to check for consistency and fairness of applying the admission criteria. He gave us a clean bill of health, and, contrary to what outsiders may have expected, some appeals were upheld by the panels because an appellant's daughter met the criteria.

No school will be free of complaints, but care must be taken that governors do not undermine the authority of the headteacher while at the same time remembering that they are accountable to parents. If a parent does complain to a governor directly one way around this problem is to ask that a letter is sent to the headteacher. This means that if a parent really has not got a justification for making the complaint, the matter will go no further. If they have a real complaint a plain statement in writing tends to prevent an over-reaction on either side, and makes the headteacher's task of investigating the complaint more straightforward. On the whole it is better if a parent's name is not divulged when an investigation is necessary and for governors not to become involved so that they are neutral to hear any appeal that may arise. It is important that governors have a mechanism for monitoring the number and types of complaint. If there is a high level of complaint about the school meals service, this could indicate that the service is not generally fulfilling expectations and the contract may need to go back out to tender rather than just be renewed at the end of the current contract period. Similarly, if complaints are continually received about a particular subject, governors may wish to have a report from external advisers on the quality of provision in that subject. However, governors must guard against becoming paranoid about a few complaints ranging from dustbins to speech days.

FINANCE AND ADMINISTRATION

The successful operation of a grant-maintained school's budget, the school administration, the contract arrangements, the personnel function and the health and safety requirements are as important to the school as the delivery of the curriculum and the welfare of its pupils. The school will not be fulfilling its duty if departmental accounts always appear overspent when they are not, if staff salaries are not paid on time and the buildings are not properly cleaned.

As a consequence many schools have put a deputy headteacher in charge of these functions and upgraded the school secretary to support these functions. Others have appointed a bursar who may have accounting qualifications. Schools may need to review this aspect of their management structure when they find it is not the best use of a deputy headteacher's time, skills and expertise, and that the upgraded school secretary cannot cope without such support. Equally, an accountant may spend too much time on budgetary matters to the exclusion of other equally important items such as ensuring proper site maintenance and meeting health and safety requirements.

What is important is that whoever is appointed must have the confidence of the headteacher and governors and particularly those holding office, they must be able to work with all the staff, both teaching and non-teaching, and have sufficient authority to be able to assume proper responsibility. Our chief administrative officer is paid at around deputy headteacher level and is neither a qualified teacher nor an accountant. However, as an experienced company secretary she is able to handle payroll, contracts, health and safety, and personnel matters. The person appointed to this kind of post is likely also to be the clerk to the governors and, as such, one of the key tasks will be to provide governors with easily understood information ranging from budget monitoring to the planned maintenance programme.

Finally, the process of tendering will be another new experience for governors, particularly the opening and recording of tenders on a due date and time. For major contracts one governor ought to be present, if not the chair or vice-chairperson.

PERSONNEL AND HEALTH AND SAFETY

This area also brings changes to the governors' responsibilities and their relation with staff. This function has previously been largely undertaken by the LEA except for appointments and some stages in the disciplinary procedure. The full personnel function covers the recruitment, selection and appointment of staff, staff review and development, discipline and grievance procedures, equal opportunities, staffing levels including restructuring, redundancy and premature retirement.

While the duties of governors will be much the same over the appointment of staff, and probably confined to senior appointments, it may be necessary to review staffing structures when vacancies occur against the school's development plan, as there is a tendency to replace like with like and miss an opportunity to forward an important part of the development plan. It may also be worth considering a wider range of selection techniques than just the half-hour interview, and here governors may have expertise to put at the disposal of the school.

Staff review will impact on the governors in two ways. First, as the headteacher has to be appraised by two people, one of whom must be a headteacher of a school in a similar situation, the governing body will have to commission these appraisers and brief them, and they in turn will provide the chairperson with a copy of their appraisal. Second, in the case of a headteacher challenging the outcome of his or her appraisal the governing body will have to appoint two reviewing officers who have not been involved previously in the process. This is also the case for deputy headteachers who have been appraised by their headteacher.

The headteacher organises an appraiser for every other teacher, but the governing body may decide that the headteacher will appoint two appraisers for each deputy headteacher. The governors will therefore not be involved in these appraisals but will undoubtedly want the headteacher to make a report when each cycle is completed, possibly highlighting particular staff development needs.

In many cases, grant-maintained schools will modify existing LEA conditions of service, disciplinary and grievance procedures but will have to come to a decision as to how far they are going to move away from national pay and conditions of service. Even the Teachers' Pay and Conditions Act No. 2 allows grant-maintained schools to opt out of the system being proposed for pay settlements. Certainly, if performance-related pay is being considered the governing body will have to set specific targets for the headteacher. This will also have to be done for appraisal, but here the targets may be more subjective. In both cases they will need to relate to the school's business plan. During the first year, governors can use the restructuring grant, SPG(R), to reduce staffing levels or restructure the organisation, preferably by premature retirement rather than redundancy. This is not an easy exercise and there is a lot of pressure on governors to reduce the number of experienced staff and replace them with newly qualified teachers to reduce the salary bill. Care must be taken to keep a balance between experience and young teachers with fresh ideas and commitment.

All schools should have a health and safety policy and an equal opportunities policy. In both cases they should be more than words on paper and all staff should be made aware of them and adhere to them. The DES capital programme has placed health and safety high on its list of priorities as this has frequently, together with maintenance, been underfunded by LEAs.

CAPITAL PROGRAMME AND SITES AND BUILDINGS

It is good practice for governors to establish a rolling programme of capital works with the headteacher as part of the school's business plan. This will take time and governors may need professional help. Capital grants from the DES are limited and, to bring projects forward, governors may have to consider other ways of raising funds or consider leasing arrangements which some companies are now offering for equipment as well as buildings.

CONCLUDING COMMENTS

In this chapter I have tried to give an overview of the changes in role and responsibility of governors of grant-maintained schools with particular reference to the management of the schools and relations with the staff. Drawing on my experience as a chairman of governors of a grant-maintained school, I have endeavoured to highlight the differences between the responsibilities of the governing body and those of the school's senior management team.

Chapter 8

Managing staff development in a grant-maintained school

Jennifer Morris, Headteacher of Southfield School in Kettering describes the management of staff development in a grant-maintained school. Southfield School opted out in April 1990. In this chapter she demonstrates the freedom of a school determining its in-service programme. This is initially described in terms of staff development with an emphasis on teaching staff. This school-based programme is centred on the role of the professional tutor in Southfield School. While this approach is practised in many LMS schools, it is early days for grant-maintained schools and the case study demonstrates how school-based staff development is moving. The way in which the personnel function may be enhanced in the future as schools become more experienced in self-management is discussed in Chapter 11.

THE CASE STUDY – SOUTHFIELD SCHOOL

The achievement of independence focuses one's mind quite dramatically on a great many issues: budgeting, catering, admissions, relationships with governors and the community, building maintenance, cleaning, to name only a few. Within the excitement of negotiating contracts, establishing new procedures and responding to multi-coloured paper from the DES, it is easy to overlook that most vital component, the staff, who, when the euphoria dies away may well ask 'was it worth it?'.

For the first time in the experience of many of us we found ourselves in the enviable position of actually employing not only teaching staff, but catering, cleaning, maintenance and support staff. In some schools the family of employees doubled almost overnight. From having a concern on a limited basis for only teaching and clerical staff we now assumed real responsibility for everyone who worked in or around the school. It seemed a fairly simple matter merely to transfer a contract of employment as it stood from the employing authority to the governors; however, as time progressed, it became clear that it was not quite so easy to administer contracts which had layer after layer of local agreements attached to them, many of which were only discovered the hard way. The excitement of achieving grant-maintained status generated a great deal of good will on all sides, but the maintenance of that good will was a challenge which could not be evaded. The sense of ownership and community which existed at that time was too good and too significant to be dissipated by careless management, indifferent treatment or lack of imagination.

It is a tribute to the professionalism of all involved in education that vast quantities of time, effort and expertise are frequently expended on the establishment of complex structures dedicated to the care of students. It is reasonable to say that, in any school, the vast majority of teachers put the pupils first in any consideration. Yet, all too frequently, little or no attention is paid to the welfare of those administering this care. Our professional jargon is full of the vocabulary of caring, supporting and encouraging – as applied to pupils – but our staff are often referred to as mere human resources to be deployed or developed as we see fit. This Olympian disregard for the people within the education system is further demonstrated by the treatment meted out by governments and public alike with the eager support of the media. It is a sorry reflection on educational management that, within school too, the assumption is often made that the carers can look after themselves – an unfortunate attitude indeed at a time when sweeping and complex changes are making extraordinary demands on staff at all levels and stress is in danger of becoming an almost acceptable occupational hazard for teachers.

The independence we had sought and achieved now gave us direct accountability not only to our governors and parents but to our professional colleagues as well. We could do little to inhibit the rate of change demanded by government, but we felt we could do a great deal to mitigate the stress factors inherent within this programme of change.

ESTABLISHING A PROFESSIONAL TUTOR POST

The most significant step in this direction was the development of the role of professional tutor. The James Report made this recommendation in 1972, but as with all reforms likely to cost money, the suggestion had been met with only a half-hearted response. I was aware that many authorities had not responded at all and was therefore both pleased and relieved to discover when I first went to Southfield that a professional tutor was already in existence. The fact that she was also pastoral deputy with a whole school responsibility for the girls' welfare and the entire pastoral system did not give her a great deal of spare time. The budget she managed was minute and the opportunities for staff development were limited within the boundaries of the county inspectorate's perception of need and their ability to seize funds and allocate them as they thought fit.

Nevertheless the experience and expertise were there, coupled with enormous enthusiasm, so I felt confident that the role could and would be developed. Previous experience made me all too aware that usually, on those rare occasions when headteachers had been encouraged to consider the role of the professional tutor, INSET co-ordination had been handed out almost to the first person unlucky enough to come along the corridor at the time. Insufficient discussion, information and funding meant that for busy headteachers the appointment of an INSET co-ordinator was just one more chore added to the mass jobs already in existence. Yet the role of the professional tutor as a refinement of the role of INSET co-ordinator is not one that can be handled by just anybody. Appointments at any level are important, but the professional tutor is crucial to the right development of the personnel function, and a good professional tutor is hard to come by. In fact, it is easier to describe what you don't want:

- Insufficient school-based experience. The professional tutor must understand how schools function at a practical and philosophical level.
- Inappropriate personal philosophy of education. A professional tutor who is not in tune with the ethos of your school can only be destructive.
- Lack of commitment to the belief that staff *deserve* to feel valued and senior management should encourage and build their self-esteem.
- Poor interpersonal skills. The professional tutor should be a communicator and listener *par excellence*.
- Lack of sensitivity. The professional tutor should be able to distinguish between what is said and what is meant; between what is real and what is perceived; between genuine concern and mere sentimentality; between caring and prying.
- Poor or little creativity. The professional tutor must be able to view an initiative in its infancy and envisage it as a policy, complete with trained staff, resources and evaluative processes and criteria – then visualise the programme to achieve this – then make it happen.
- Poor organisational skills. Training days can be nightmares if arrangements are slovenly.
- Little personal authority or charisma. There is no need for the professional tutor to be Wonder Woman or Superman, but an invisible personality is no help for a position of professional leadership.
- Poor appreciation or understanding of the nature of professionalism. Whatever else, the professional tutor must be the true professional, at all times acting as an example for others. Anything less will diminish the confidence all members of staff need to be able to feel in the person who is advising them.
- Lack of discretion. A professional tutor who cannot be trusted is a contradiction in terms.

PROVIDING THE APPROPRIATE ENVIRONMENT AND STATUS

We knew, thankfully, that we had the right person and the role was about to be developed. The next problem to be solved was one of resources, as always.

The basic requirements of an office, a desk and a lockable filing cabinet were already in existence, but it was felt appropriate to add some easy chairs, a coffee table and the means of producing tea and coffee easily. The only problem was that the office currently in use was right in the heart of the administration area, the last place to go for a quiet conversation. Hence, with the aid of the transition grant the office was moved into an area of the school which, though still central, was more likely to yield an uninterrupted opportunity for concentration and discussion.

The other two essentials for the post were time and status. If either were missing the effects might well be the opposite of those desired. The reality is, as always, that nothing comes from nothing and this was one initiative which could not be achieved by the judicious use of a yoghurt pot, glue and an egg box. Teachers are used to being short-changed as far as salary and resources are concerned but a professional tutor with forty minutes per week and a B incentive allowance to look after their interests is an affront to their professional and personal development. The philosophy that expresses a genuine concern for staff cannot be embraced half-heartedly, but the profit gained from a realistic investment of time and resources will far outweigh any apparent sacrifices.

In order to provide the appropriate time for the professional tutor to devote to staff development, her other main responsibility, that of the pastoral care for pupils, was delegated to the heads of lower, middle and upper school and one of the first areas of concentration was staff development for the three members of staff concerned. Their response was gratifying; not only did they welcome the training but they welcomed the opportunities that were given to them to establish a real role and a genuine responsibility within the school. This meant that our professional tutor now had a little more 'elbow room' in which to consider and organise the development of her now most significant area of responsibility.

One of her most urgent tasks was consideration of a whole-school staff development policy. This was already in existence, but it related specifically to a school within the constraints of an LEA. A grant-maintained school, however, is in the unique position of being able not only to develop such a policy independently but to implement it in a way which is of specific value to that particular establishment.

MANAGING FUNDS

All too frequently, schools have been very well aware of their needs, but the means to meet those needs have been controlled by others, whose perceptions of required training and its delivery have often been widely at variance. The quantity of paperwork could vary from LEA to LEA and from complex to mind-crushing; and the labyrinths of some LEA INSET offices and procedures required a Ph.D. in geography and psychology to negotiate. Out of this had come the mind- and bottom-numbing training day we have all come to know and dread; the cobbled-together course delivered by an expert who had little or no conception of the effect two and a half hours of solid talk has on teachers who have been working all day, knowing that they have three hours of marking to do that evening and are desperate for a cup of tea and a soft chair. We have all known examples of the earnest advisory teacher compelled to deliver a course on a national initiative about which there was little or no information. It follows therefore that all too frequently the words training and staff development have been synonymous with crushing boredom, frustration, condescension, second-rate facilities and third-rate or non-existent refreshments. That is not the way to raise morale or instruct professionals and the carelessness with which this area has in the past been addressed by many authorities is a sad reflection on the importance that they have placed upon it. It was imperative, therefore, that we should do our utmost to counter the mistrust and cynicism related to staff development and the SPG(D) has enabled us to achieve this objective.

Bidding for this funding looked initially to be somewhat of a minefield. The instructions and information relating to the bid were, as is so frequently the case, half an inch thick and weighed several pounds. However, one soon learns to disentangle the content from the verbiage and the focus of concern was made quite clear. It was then a fairly simple matter to assemble the information that we already had regarding the training needs of staff and departments as well as whole school needs and to create a year's programme. Training related to actual needs, pleasant comfortable venues, decent refreshments and well-briefed genuinely expert providers have all served to re-establish training as a useful and meaningful experience in the minds of members of staff. Significantly, traditional and entrepreneurial providers have become aware that a poor performance will be used in evidence against them by all grant-maintained schools, and inadequate preparation and sloppy presentation is now an unusual occurrence. She who holds the cheque book calls not only the tune but also the standard of delivery! At long last trainers of all varieties and levels of experience are waking up to the reality that they are there to serve staff and not merely give them what they feel like doling out. A number of LEAs have also become aware that they too, if they wish to support their own development budgets, must give schools what they actually require. Those who leave grant-maintained schools at the end of the queue when it comes to awarding places on courses and those who fail to organise their programmes until half the year is over are simply left out of our consideration. There are courses and providers in abundance from which to choose with universities being wonderfully co-operative and creative in their response to our requests.

We were fortunate at Southfield that the essentials of both policy and practice were positively established, hitherto lacking only the funds to develop them even further. The SPG(D), however, gave us the chance we had been waiting for. It was imperative that a system be established that was clearly understood by all and could be monitored easily, in order that our needs should be clearly stated and understood and the INSET should meet those needs. Without this the situation would soon degenerate and coherent development would become impossible. This is where the professional tutor came into her own, devising practical methods of ensuring that budgetary requirements could be monitored efficiently, as well as creating simple but effective organisational procedures.

Heads of faculty were given the responsibility for the training of members of their individual teams. For some heads of faculty this was a novel concept, but one which was eagerly and quickly learned and appreciated. The difficulty lay in curbing their enthusiasm and ingenuity. The realisation was not slow to dawn that training was not only about courses, and much use was made of shadowing staff in our own and other schools as well as in industry. Visits to other establishments of all kinds and group sessions for brainstorming and discussion became almost commonplace. The capacity to invite an expert to visit a faculty and spend concentrated time with its members was initially regarded as a luxury, until it became apparent that this was in fact a highly efficient and economical use of expertise and staff time. An hour spent with a small group focusing on a specific area of concern was more effective than a whole morning spent with a large group, when presentations tend to become diffuse and discussions wander to the esoteric. In a short space of time, heads of faculty became expert in devising exciting and imaginative programmes for the development of their teams and, because they too had a hand in choosing and organising the provision, their response was positive and the effects frequently dynamic.

MANAGING THE PROCESS

The needs of individuals are by no means neglected, and every member of staff is involved in a professional review with the head of faculty, the pastoral head and the professional tutor every year. Thus the career developments and ambitions of individual members of staff are properly catered for within a framework which ensures that all needs are bound together to serve the aims of whole-school development and ultimately the good of the pupils. It came as something of a shock to realise that, for new members of staff, the idea of actually being considered as a professional person with anxieties and ambitions is an astonishing concept, but one which they welcome with tremendous enthusiasm. It is sad to consider that for many teachers the idea of appraisal or review can only be seen as threatening because that is their only experience. Questions are asked only when things go wrong and criticism is more freely handed out than praise or simple recognition of hard work. Individual aspirations are seen merely as spanners thrown into the working of the timetable. The personnel function is still non-existent in far too many establishments, and the introduction of appraisal into an environment which gives out so many other uncaring messages can be seen as hypocritical at best, and downright threatening at worst. It should be emphasised, however, that this process of establishing the right atmosphere and meeting staff needs is no small task and if it is to be done properly needs both time and expertise. Our professional tutor has plenty of both and has gained quite deservedly both the respect and trust of her colleagues who recognise the real concern she has for their well-being, as well as the support given to her both philosophically and practically by the headteacher and governing body.

The responsibilities of the professional tutor

The essential responsibilities delegated to the professional tutor are as follows:

- Preparing the bid for the SPG(D), submitting it to the DES, and obtaining approval.
- With the finance manager establishing a system which will control and monitor expenditure of SPG(D).
- Establishing and operating a system whereby heads of faculty bid for their share of development funding and monitor its expenditure.
- Establishing and operating a system whereby individual staff, both teaching and support, may request and receive assistance with their personal development.
- Ensuring that all developmental programmes are directed towards the achievement of the school aims and that they fall within the philosophical parameters of the ethos of the school.
- Establishing and overseeing a system of staff appraisal which fulfils not only those obligations designated by the Secretary of State, but also the requirements of the school and its personnel.
- The organisation and conduct of staff interviews.
- The care, induction and on-going training of probationary teachers.
- The organisation and implementation of an induction programme for all new members of staff.
- The induction and support of supply staff.
- The organisation of training where appropriate for support and clerical staff.
- Having oversight of the practice and reporting of the evaluation of departments, projects, groups, individuals and initiatives.

From this list of responsibilities it becomes clear that the professional tutor is in many respects the monitor of quality provision within the school, an extremely significant role, yet one which has not been prominent in the thinking of educational management.

These responsibilities contain a multitude of tasks, some of which may be delegated, but all of which require a clear mind, steady purpose and a first-rate capacity to organise. An encyclopaedic knowledge of course procedures does not come amiss either!

The role of the professional tutor

It was not felt appropriate for the professional tutor to become involved in staff establishment work. It is indeed desirable that the postholder should be involved in interviews for new staff and in discussions relating to internal promotions, but it was felt important that within the administration team we have a member of staff who was responsible for placing advertisements, sending out application forms, requesting references, preparing contracts, confirming salaries and qualifications and requesting police clearance. Time-sheets, overtime records, sick pay regulations, pensions enquiries, health and safety matters and employment legislation are all highly significant factors within the organisation of the school and it is important that you either engage or train your own expert at the earliest opportunity. It is not reasonable for the professional tutor to carry out such tasks, and though your finance manager may pay the salaries, it is not always appropriate for that person to keep track of contractual changes or establish conditions of service for support staff.

Great emphasis has been placed quite rightly on the successful appointment of a finance manager, but from a practical point of view the personnel function should not be neglected. When even a small school will employ teaching staff, clerical staff, technicians, caretakers, cleaners, lunch-time supervisors and possibly others, it is vitally important that someone knows the rules relating to employment and also has the ability to deal efficiently and discreetly with all the paperwork. In the world of employment litigation, good intentions are not enough to protect you and the governors from a great deal of anxiety, and even the most placid employee can become unpleasant if you unwittingly contravene rules you did not know existed. Unions too have little sympathy for employers who have not taken the trouble to protect themselves or their employees by proper procedures at the point of contractual obligation.

The psychology of good industrial relations is a constant study for those involved in industry and commerce, yet the teaching profession, whose intended product is stable, fulfilled, widely educated people, frequently ignores this crucial aspect of management, and concentrates on the management of change, or resource management. Yet the in-depth study of good relationships between managers and personnel is not only fascinating but should be an integral part of preparation for all senior postholders. Incredibly, some heads of faculty who can motivate thirty unruly, unwilling pupils to great heights of achievement and behaviour, will treat their col- leagues with indifference, tyranny, insensitivity or even downright rudeness, without seeing the contradictions inherent in their behaviour.

A close partnership between the professional tutor and senior management will clarify those issues which need to be urgently addressed as well as channelling energies and finances to those people and areas most in need of motivation or investment. There is an urgent need within education for managers at all levels actually to learn to manage. It may be considered trite to restate the obvious – that our most valuable resource is our staff – but the fact remains that people who are disgruntled, frustrated or merely bored by their jobs will not be giving of their best. The head of faculty who has by lack of inclination or training allowed such situations to develop within the team, is in serious need of training in personnel management. Consideration for staff should be an element of our professional care which permeates the establishment. It is the professional tutor who sets the tone but the ultimate responsibility rests with all of us.

The vexed question of job descriptions should be considered at this point. Some managers like to create quite specific and detailed descriptions which leave little or no room for manoeuvre; others prefer the job outline, feeling that this offers fewer constraints to those wishing to use their initiative. Whatever one's view, it is important that all staff of whatever status have some idea of one's expectations. Sensibly the professional tutor may have a contribution to make to the job description of teaching staff, at least by making certain that they all have one! It is equally sensible that the job specifications of support staff should be established by someone who knows, understands and has responsibility for what they are doing, and is therefore in a position to evaluate performance and recommend training, salary increases, promotion or a change of role.

The role of support staff

The appointment of an administration manager to deal with staff establishment matters is a godsend to the headteacher who is grappling with catering, maintenance, capital grants and all the other non-educational issues as well as the curriculum. This is also an excellent opportunity to appraise the work of support staff, with regard not only to efficiency, but to necessity and direction. Over a period of time, systems, or lack of them, become entrenched in school offices, especially when the controlling authority is particularly proscriptive. The chance to create procedures which actually serve the convenience of the school community is too good to be missed.

This is also the time to consider those tasks currently undertaken by teaching staff and possibly reassign a number of them to clerical or other support staff. After all, there is no tablet of stone which states that supply cover must be arranged by a member of the teaching staff and few managers in industry would expect to do their own filing – an everyday occurrence for deputy heads and sometimes headteachers as well. It is financially and philosophically satisfying to pass mundane but necessary tasks from relatively highly paid teachers to less expensive support staff, who are frequently more efficient at them, thus relieving teachers of the irritations of list-compiling or counting photograph money and giving them more freedom and time to do the job for which they are best qualified. It makes no sense for a head of faculty to be taking stock and making booklists when one clerical/general assistant can service the day-to-day administrative needs of several departments, thus enabling managers to manage, and teachers to teach. An overhaul of the entire support structure can yield excellent dividends in efficiency, cost effectiveness and mitigation of stress.

MONITORING AND EVALUATING THE WORK OF THE TEACHING STAFF

The corporate health of any establishment requires consistent and effective monitoring, if whole-school development is to be coherent. Evaluation of individual, departmental and whole-school performance needs to be structured accordingly to a programme which yields accurate information when it is most needed. Performance indicators are no use if they are six months out of date or the data are unavailable when required. In addition, an appraisal system which supports and encourages the professional development of staff, requires careful planning and implementation. These activities need to be organised by staff trained and experienced enough to maximise both opportunities and effects. The development and stability of the school and its staff are too precious to be left to chance and a professional tutor is ideally placed to take overall responsibility for the implementation of these major initiatives.

NEW RECRUITS TO THE TEACHING PROFESSION

The training for students and the induction of probationary teachers are significant areas of responsibility which must not be left in limbo. As centres of excellence, grant-maintained schools must aspire to staff who will be the educational leaders of the future. To this end it is important that we invest both time and expertise in order to demonstrate to the public and to the government of the day that members of staff of grant-maintained schools are the cream of the crop. There are currently many doubts regarding the quality of teacher training and these anxieties must be laid to rest by sound induction and further development programmes which guarantee a first-class entry into the profession for all probationary teachers.

STAFF RESTRUCTURING IN THE SCHOOL

If all else fails, then there is of course the SPG(R) which offers an opportunity for the headteacher and governors to consider a change of management and organisation structure, by funding early retirement with compensation. This opportunity does not exist for ever. Any member or members of staff who may be considered to be appropriate for the receipt of such bounty must be considered within the first year of incorporation. The actual retirement need not take place until the second year, but plans have to originate within that first year and application made to the DES for approval. This funding support is invaluable as it offers what may well be the last opportunity for the restructuring of the school organisation. In the future it is highly unlikely that governors will countenance the expenditure of vast sums to support early retirement.

CONCLUSION

We may state publicly that our most precious asset is our staff, but the real significance of our statement lies in the way in which they are treated. Decent working conditions, clean toilets, quiet staffrooms and clean and pleasant work areas are hardly luxuries, yet they are often at the bottom of the school shopping list. To those who consider the expenditure of funds on new staffroom furniture as wilfully extravagant I would suggest that curriculum development is only as sound as the staff who are implementing the policies. Low morale in staff achieves headlines all too frequently, and may be attributable to many factors, but at the heart of them all lies teachers' perception of being generally undervalued. There will be total amazement on the day a national daily paper prints a realistic and factual appraisal of the standard achieved by teachers in conditions most workforces would reject out of hand. Those of us who know the truth should endeavour to counter the chilly wind of ill-informed criticism from outside the profession by warm appreciation from within. We are quick to respond to such symptoms as underachievement and low self-esteem in our pupils. It is just as important to make certain that our professional colleagues do not suffer in the same way.

All grant-maintained schools are very much concerned that inadequate training, high levels of stress or poor working conditions will be seen, quite rightly, as management failure. There is no one else to blame but ourselves if such conditions exist. We are no longer able to blame the faceless ones in county hall. This is the price of independence. Yet caring for staff both physically and intellectually makes sound business sense. If you take as a performance indicator the amount of absenteeism within your establishment, you will discover very rapidly precisely what funds may be saved by the development of a personnel function. It is sound business sense to keep staff not only busy but happy in their work; and if this means paying for tea and coffee at breaktime, giving them decent seats in which to sit and tidy desks at which to work, and concerned managers who are involved with their own development and that of others, then this investment should be high on the agenda of all headteachers and governors.

Part III

Part II.

Chapter 9

The advantages of grant-maintained status

The advantages of being a self-managing school centre around the general attributes of self-management and those that focus on the particular nature of obtaining the status of and operating as a grant-maintained school. The former can be considered as the fundamental arguments for self-management, while the latter are concerned with the particular financial inducements and benefits associated with the move to grant-maintained status provided by a government seeking to encourage schools to opt out. This chapter seeks to outline both these sets of advantages and then reflect on the evidence of the six case studies to assess whether, at this early stage, they have become apparent in practice.

The advantages of becoming a grant-maintained school can be seen in the following areas:

- freedom for the school to make its own decisions
- targeting resources to educational goals
- the opportunity to restructure and rethink
- more effective decision-making
- increased accountability
- increased resources
- increased parental and pupil commitment

FREEDOM FOR THE SCHOOL TO MAKE ITS OWN DECISIONS

The proponents of decentralisation have long argued that, for effective decision-making, it is vital for decisions to be delegated to the most appropriate decision-making unit that comes into contact with the client. It is those in day-to-day contact with the clients who know their needs and can make decisions that maximise resource use, and not remotely sited managers who make decisions without that informed perspective. In the educational world, the National Curriculum's key stages provide an appropriate framework on which to base decisions about resource requirements. The delivery of the curriculum within this framework is more effectively achieved if those with the practical responsibility for it have the freedom to make choices thereby enabling them to maximise the educational provision by using their detailed practical knowledge and experience. It is the individual school which is best placed to make these judgements about the most appropriate mix of resources that will meet the educational needs of its children.

Schools vary in their needs, as do different cohorts of children, so that a different mix of resources will be required by different schools and also within the same school with different groups of children. This sort of flexibility has not been possible with traditional, centralised LEA systems where resources have been allocated in predetermined categories. Even under LMS schemes LEAs still retain funds that the school may wish to spend in alternative ways to maximise its particular educational productivity.

The complete freedom to choose the providers and suppliers of all the services and products that are required enhances the school's ability to meet more precisely its specific needs. The freedom extends from employing teachers to educational supplies and floor maintenance equipment. Additionally, this encourages competition and initiative in the educational suppliers' network that services the educational world, replacing the monopoly position of the LEA.

It is not only this freedom to determine the resource mix and use of appropriate suppliers that provides an advantage to grant-maintained schools, it is also the freedom from LEA bureaucracy. The ability to make decisions can only be valued if they can quickly and effectively be turned into action. Schools have previously complained about delays in decision-making by bureaucratic LEAs that have resulted in decisions taking weeks and often months to implement. Local authority control mechanisms and purchasing policies have added both time and frustration as an additional management burden that a school has to bear. Freed from this control, schools can move quickly and efficiently to activate and implement their decisions.

TARGETING RESOURCES TO MEET EDUCATIONAL GOALS

Since the 1988 ERA the educational framework has put a significantly increased emphasis on both school development planning and measures of outputs from schools. This change of emphasis can be seen by considering the following model of education:

$$\text{INPUT} \quad \Rightarrow \quad \text{PROCESS} \quad \Rightarrow \quad \text{OUTPUT}$$

Whereas previously schools had little or no control over inputs, they had considerable autonomy over the curriculum and methodology they employed which meant that outputs, apart from examination results, were generalised and often disputed.

The 1988 ERA changed this framework to one where the process is determined by the National Curriculum and output by pupil assessment at the four key age stages of 7, 11, 14 and 16, together with individual schools developing their own organisational performance indicators. How schools are to deliver the National Curriculum and meet the output targets they set themselves provides the challenge for school management in the 1990s. To meet this challenge the flexibility in deploying resources and specifically targeting them to meet defined organisational goals is the vital component that grant-maintained status offers. This does, of course, provide a very specific accountability for grant-maintained schools; if they control the resources and the National Curriculum goals are built into their school development plan, what remains for them is to deliver it! The way schools achieve this depends on how they change from an incremental deployment of resources based on previous allocation patterns to a zero-based approach which targets resources to defined output goals. This is the central focus of self-managing schools.

THE OPPORTUNITY TO RESTRUCTURE AND RETHINK

Freed from LEA control, schools have the fundamental opportunity to reappraise how they are organised and what their organisational mission is. Whilst it is evident that many of the earlier schools to opt out did so because of the threat of reorganisation or closure, choosing opting out to preserve the *status quo*, an increasing number of schools have opted for self-management in its own right and it is now apparent that the desire for organisational freedom is the predominant motive.

So, although some grant-maintained schools may not want to change and develop, others have taken the opportunity to rethink and restructure their organisation. This has been assisted in a limited way by a restructuring grant, SPG(R), which is provided by the DES as part of the support arrangements during the early years of grant-maintained status.

If schools are to maximise fully the potential of grant-maintained status then they need to take advantage of the opportunity to be different. Neither merely preserving the existing *status quo* nor using extra finance are significant responses to the challenge of self-management. Schools need to consider the fundamental issues of how they redefine their mission, allocate resources and above all maximise pupil learning and achievement. Assuming this can be done by replicating the past and not examining alternatives made possible by the new framework is a wasted opportunity. Schools should be different as they seek alternative methods to achieve the best for their children.

MORE EFFECTIVE DECISION-MAKING

The fact that the school is responsible for all its own decisions means that there is the opportunity for greater involvement by all staff and governors.

However, the danger is that one person's decentralisation is another person's centralisation. If decentralisation to the school results in more power being centralised with the headteacher and governors and no effective decision-making being decentralised within the school, then staff will lack motivation and involvement. Management in schools needs to be perceived not just is a line management function, but also as a function that promotes common values and goals so that individuals are encouraged to make a contribution and are fully involved in organising their professional life. A better model of this type of management could be considered as a partnership of governors, headteacher, staff and pupils.

How far individual teachers can be involved in deciding the best way to combine resources to meet the educational needs of their pupils will determine whether self-management empowers teachers with a new sense of professional involvement or treats them as employees carrying out orders from above. If the rationale for grant-maintained schools centres around the belief that those closer to the client are better able to make decisions than those remote from the process, it must follow that those in day-to-day contact with the children have the immediate knowledge that can contribute to effective decision-making. Sadly, the AMMA report of their questionnaire survey (Appendix D pp. 156–64) suggests that little change in management style is evident yet. The replication of this limited type of involvement in a larger number of schools over a period of time could lead to staff feeling alienated from the new managerialism and the opportunity to foster new staff involvement and shared decision-making may be lost.

By contrast, the American experience of decentralised management is based on shared decision-making where the teachers have to agree how resources are to be reallocated in order to attempt to increase the learning outcome of their pupils. Unless the teachers vote to be involved in the process it does not happen. Encouragingly, the American experience to date shows that whenever they are given the choice teachers have taken the opportunity to enhance their professional involvement and increase their effectiveness. It is interesting that a bottom-up approach in the USA has been ignored in favour of a top-down approach in this country. It is our belief that, if self- managing schools are to be effective in the long run, then real involvement and ownership by the teachers is vital for the health of the organisation and success in pupil achievement.

INCREASED ACCOUNTABILITY

Accountability in grant-maintained schools is addressed in two ways: the formal accountability and market accountability. The first, formal accountability, may be considered to be both national and local. In national terms the school's accountability responsibilities are to the Secretary of State for Education and Science through the DES. Additionally, the activities of grant-maintained schools are subject to inspection by Her Majesty's

Inspectorate of Schools in the same way that LEA schools are monitored.

On the local level, one dimension of accountability is provided through the structure of the governing body (details are provided in Chapter 2). Parent, teacher and local community representatives on the governing body ensure that the interests of all parties are addressed. Another aspect of local accountability is obtained through the governors' legal responsibilities of reporting annually to the parents of the pupils at the school. This entails an annual report and an annual parents' meeting. Parents also have the opportunity, as does any interested party, to complain to the Secretary of State if they believe that a governing body is acting unreasonably in using its powers, or is failing to carry out its duties properly. If the Secretary of State agrees that the complaint is justified, he can direct the governing body to take whatever action seems to him to be appropriate.

Market accountability, as outlined in Chapter 1, arises out of the formula funding method of allocating finance to the school and, at the same time, is linked to open enrolment. If the school provides the education parents want, then it will attract pupils and hence funds. If it fails to deliver the necessary quality of education parents will choose other schools and the funding will follow the pupils. Thus, the school has the ultimate accountability dimension, that of survival, to motivate it to provide a quality education for its pupils.

More effective school-based accountability is likely to emerge; for example, the state of the art after two years of grant-maintained schools is that a grant-maintained school quality assurance voluntary code of practice has been drawn up and governing bodies are being consulted. Subscription to this by the governors of a grant-maintained school is a public declaration of their statement of intent to ensure that there is a regular cycle of evaluation within their school. This includes both a continuous process of internal evaluation and a planned cycle of external evaluation carried out by independent outside bodies. The details of the policy statement are left for each individual governing body to determine. The code requires the governing body to publish its commitment to such evaluation in the school prospectus, publish a summary of the external evaluations and actions consequent upon it in the annual report to parents, and register the fact and date of each external evaluation, together with the identity of the evaluators and a summary of the report and response with an independent agency, for example, the Grant-Maintained Schools' Foundation. The details of the code of practice are given in Appendix C. This approach seems to be supported by recent statements by Kenneth Clarke, Secretary of State for Education and Science.

INCREASED RESOURCES

The often cited reason for opting out and becoming a grant-maintained school is that it increases the resources available to the school. At the time of writing, grant-maintained schools receive funding through the following grants:

- A one-off transitional grant to assist with the costs incurred in preparation for grant-maintained status.
- An annual maintenance grant (AMG) based on the LMS formula developed by the school's former LEA plus 16 per cent.
- Special purpose grants to cover staff development, staff restructuring (another one-off payment that schools can only apply for during their first year of grant-maintained status) and the additional VAT for which the governors of a grant-maintained school are liable.
- Capital allocations which comes in two parts: a formula-funded grant and the opportunity to bid annually for a grant relating to particular projects.

Compared with a school under the LMS system, a grant-maintained school would appear to benefit in terms of revenue, although it has to meet the increased additional costs of services that were previously provided by the LEA as well as addressing some of the adverse economies of scale in purchasing services and products on an individual school basis. For example, in some respects economies of scale are lost when in-service training and staff development are organised by a single school.

The relative size of capital allocation for major building work for grant-maintained schools has been one of the main points of attack by the critics of the system. For example, the *Observer* reported in an article entitled 'Strathclyde set to close over 80 schools in ruins' (18 August 1991) with regard to building maintenance: 'On average, a CTC receives 80 times more than an ordinary school, and opt-out schools four times as much.' Whilst it is true that some of the early grant-maintained schools benefited considerably by this funding arrangement, it is not true for all grant-maintained schools and indeed raises some questions about the way in which capital funding has been allocated within the sector. Indeed, at the time of writing, it has just become known that, in preparation for the 1992 capital bid, the DES is preparing more detailed information on the criteria used for allocating capital grants. It is interesting to speculate whether this level of funding will continue as more schools opt out and achieve grant-maintained status.

INCREASED PARENTAL AND PUPIL COMMITMENT

The fact that parents have to become involved in the decision-making process by voting in a ballot as to whether their school should seek grant-maintained status engenders considerable commitment to the school. In doing this the parents are expressing a positive commitment to having their children educated in a grant-maintained school. This is reinforced by the choice of that school for their children to attend compared with the alternatives that are provided by the LEA and not selected by parents. Early evidence from grant-maintained schools has shown that the majority of them have experienced a considerable increase in the number of applications for school places.

This parental commitment also has considerable impact on the pupils' attitude to the school and their commitment to it. When parents take an interest in their children's schooling, both in terms of the individual's learning and in the general life and workings of the school, it is then viewed by the children as a normal part of their daily lives with their parents playing an active role in their education. The values and ethos of the school are shared and understood by the parents and are likely to be reinforced for the children by them. All of this increases the children's understanding of the school and what it is trying to achieve. This, in turn, is likely to improve the pupils' attitude and commitment to the school.

REFLECTIONS ON CURRENT PRACTICE

How these advantages are reflected in practice needs a long-term study of a significant number of grant-maintained schools. The case studies in Part II can provide some pointers.

In Chapter 3 Cecil Knight makes the statement, 'Grant-maintained status in itself does not create a successful educational enterprise. What counts is using the flexibility and greater control of resources wisely and purposefully, according to a well-defined educational philosophy'. Later he goes on to suggest that it 'offered a unique opportunity ... to work in a new and potentially more effective and creative manner'. Accepting the challenge of the new grant-maintained framework is apparent in statements such as 'using the financial freedom to enable the school to provide the education that it believes is appropriate' (Keith Barker, in Chapter 5). This demonstrates that schools are concerned with reassessing how productivity can be increased. The contributors provide numerous examples of how they have used different resource combinations to enhance the provision in their schools and the advantages of flexibility are very apparent.

Certainly the funds previously held centrally by the LEA have been directed to the teaching and learning process. This has led to some spectacular increases in capitation and staffing; for example, Roger Perks talks about increasing capitation by 600 per cent and employing six extra teachers as well as an additional secretary. The other contributors provide their own similar accounts of spending. Thus, there is considerable evidence of increased resources for these schools which in itself is a very powerful stimulus to improved educational performance.

On the grounds of flexibility there is evidence of considerable advantages for the schools but how this is increasing productivity in terms of student performance is probably too early to determine. Accountability in market terms from the evidence of Baverstock seems significantly improved.

Chapter 10

The disadvantages of grant-maintained status

The disadvantages of schools obtaining grant-maintained status can be considered from two perspectives: that of the effect on the education system as a whole and that of the effect on the management at the individual school level.

THE EDUCATION SYSTEM PERSPECTIVE

Looking at the broader effects on the education system and schools in general, a number of points can be highlighted:

- diseconomies of scale
- inappropriateness of market forces in education
- difficulties in coherent planning
- reducing equality of opportunity
- a covert move back to selection
- lack of accountability and monitoring
- reduced funding as more schools opt out
- political uncertainty

Diseconomies of scale

These can be considered in two ways. First, in the traditional financial and economic sense, large organisations, because of their size and buying power, can obtain goods at significantly lower prices through discounting. Additionally, the size an organisation has to be to provide efficient and economic services, such as school psychological services, legal and financial systems, advisory support and many others, suggests that the individual school is too small as a unit and it would seem that a non-profit-making organisation, such as an LEA, should be able to co-ordinate and organise these services at a lower cost than schools having to deal individually with profit-making firms.

Second, economies of scale can be considered in an intellectual sense. By pooling the experience of up to eighty secondary schools or over two hundred primary schools, an LEA can organise a mechanism for sharing new ideas and good practice that keeps all schools informed. The danger is that schools outside this network can become impoverished by the lack of this opportunity. Additionally, if we consider the training and development provided to employees in the commercial world, it is the large international companies which tend to have more highly developed training schemes for their staff. The smaller units often ignore training and recruit staff from the larger firms once they have been trained. Whether this pattern will be repeated in the school sector remains to be seen. LEAs could train and develop staff by bringing pressure to bear on the school, which if left to its own devices, would not become involved. This intellectual isolation may be avoided, but it is difficult to predict whether this will happen at this stage in the life of grant-maintained schools.

Inappropriateness of market forces in education

Market forces may be an inappropriate method of evaluating or running an education system. While the school may pursue policies that benefit it individually, these may result in significant disadvantages for the local community. This is particularly true in an open enrolment situation. Planned provision that looks after the interests of all the children may become increasingly difficult within this environment. Short-term marketing may attract pupils to one school, closing others, but once closed that provision may not be available elsewhere or the popular school may be in an inappropriate geographical location. It may be better to improve the less popular school and retain balance and comprehensive provision in the system.

This last point can be developed to show that a market mechanism may not be the most effective way of providing a national education system. In an educational service controlled by market mechanisms parents and children are seen as the clients. As such they have educational wants and needs. Wants in this context can be defined as what the clients perceive that they want from the school and how far they perceive the school is delivering it. However, there may be a different set of educational needs that society at large or professional educators include within their list of desired requirements from the education service. A market system responds in its resource allocation to the client's wants, which they demonstrate through their choice, although these could be detrimental to meeting the more significant educational needs.

Difficulties in coherent planning

This can be assessed from a number of viewpoints. At local level, whilst there are only a few grant-maintained schools, LEAs can still make adequate local provision. Once more than 15 to 20 per cent of the schools have opted out,

LEAs have less resources and are affected by diseconomies of scale, and it becomes difficult for them to make effective provision for the remaining schools as the costs rise proportionally. Also, although schools are taken out of local authority control, the debt the authority incurred in building them remains with the LEA thereby further limiting the resource base and inhibiting the ability to make coherent provision within the area through lack of funds. In the long term it is likely to pose problems in motivating LEAs to build schools, the control of which they may lose very quickly.

On a national level, the ability of the DES to deal directly and efficiently with 200 grant-maintained schools does present them with an organisational problem, but one that is manageable. However, the existence of thousands of opted out schools will call for a more radical approach to the arrangements for servicing them and it is suggested that either a central bureaucracy or some sort of regional organisation is likely to be necessary. If a regional approach is adopted the situation could arise where LEAs are re-invented but controlled by central government patronage rather than local, democratically elected government. Yet unless regionally co-ordinated, this fragmented system could make it difficult for central government to implement policy as, to date, it has relied on LEAs to implement and check compliance. Whether central government can efficiently monitor what is happening in each school individually is a question that remains to be answered.

Reducing equality of opportunity

Choice as a concept is seductive, but to be more than this it needs to be turned into effective choice. Grammar schools and those that were formerly selective in middle-class suburbs can find that choice works for them as their clients make informed choices and, where necessary, can make the financial contribution to transport their children from the immediate neighbourhood school to one in the desired location.

However, what of the child in a poor inner-city school? What pressures are there to improve that child's education? In this situation, informed parental choice about educational options may be absent, as is likely to be the financial ability to transport children to other schools even if a choice could be made. There is little evidence to date that suggests that the grant-maintained schools are improving the opportunities for the lower socio-economic groups and rather more evidence that the *status quo* is being maintained. There is a danger, in fact, that opting out may increase the differentiation and create a two-tier system consisting of those schools in the more prosperous areas which have opted out because of parental interest and a group of 'sink' inner-city schools run by a diminished LEA. A really radical solution to this problem would be to require all grant-maintained schools to take at least 25 per cent of their intake from lower socio-economic groups to try to equalise out educational opportunity.

A covert move back to selection

A high proportion of schools opting out during the first two years of grant-maintained status were selective schools and the ability of schools to petition the Secretary of State for a change of character is considered by some as evidence of a covert move back to a type of grammar school selection. This is significant because the greater the variety of schools in an area the more difficult it becomes for there to be a coherent pattern of provision. Making the argument that it is possible to have comprehensive schools side-by-side with grammar schools and still maintain parity of esteem or even a comprehensive intake for the comprehensive school is difficult to take seriously, even for the most ardent supporter of diversity of provision! This is demonstrated by the severe problems LEAs have experienced when opted out, single-sex grammar schools have increased their intake. By law the LEA is required to provide equal opportunities from a gender perspective, yet building more grammar schools may destroy its planned comprehensive provision within the area. The result is a no-win situation for the authority in terms of its planned provision and, possibly, a great deal of animosity.

Lack of accountability and monitoring

As more schools have opted out it has become clear that, in the planning stages, insufficient consideration has been paid to the effective monitoring and accountability dimensions of their status. Although the theory suggests that their survival is in the hands of market forces, there are serious doubts as to whether this mechanism could provide effective educational evaluation at anything other than a superficial level. Additionally it is not possible or appropriate for HMI to take on this role given its present remit, the limitations of its staffing and the uncertainty about its future role. Yet, as they are state schools, the government has a responsibility to ensure that grant-maintained schools are delivering an effective education and they cannot ignore this for long. The grant-maintained schools themselves have drawn up a voluntary code of practice for quality assurance (see Appendix C, pp. 154–5). Compared to the accountability of a democratically elected local authority this may be considered a rather inadequate form of accountability.

Reduced funding as more schools opt out

The level of financial provision and inducements given to schools to opt out in the early years would require a significant expansion in public expenditure on education if replicated on a large scale as more schools seek the status. With current government policy wishing to keep public expenditure controlled, it is unlikely that this level of support would continue. Central funding of education on any scale would be likely to gravitate towards a level operated by the previously lower spending LEAs rather than higher spending ones. Increased central control is likely to result in constrained, rather than expanded levels of educational spending.

Political uncertainty

Changed political control from Conservative to Labour would result in grant-maintained schools being returned to the LEA system. This level of political uncertainty gives the grant-maintained sector a difficult framework in which to plan and operate.

THE SCHOOL LEVEL PERSPECTIVE

At the school level the disadvantages inherent in being a self-managing, grant-maintained school can be seen in a number of areas:

- schools becoming insular.
- increased applications for the wrong reasons.
- grant-maintained schools as private monopolies.
- autocratic management styles.
- governors becoming managers instead of governing.
- erosion of staff rights.
- maintaining rather than developing standards.

Schools becoming insular

When a school is not part of the LEA network it can become very inward-looking and may not be exposed to the wider pressures. There is a danger of schools attempting to preserve the *status quo* and not adapting to the new challenges that face the education system. The incremental process of repeating past practice can be beneficial when replicating good practice, but obviously detrimental when ingraining bad practice into the organisational method of working or the culture. Headteachers and staff need to be open to wider influences to develop individually and organisationally. This is not a problem for schools that recognise these needs but those that ignore them face a long and slow process of becoming isolated and fossilised. Within the LEA system there would be pressure for them to change.

Increased applications for the wrong reasons

Grant-maintained schools are often perceived by the public as semi-independent schools. Parents may believe that they are getting private education for their children without having to pay fees. This misconception and the underfunding of the LEA sector may be reasons that have led to the increase in applications for places that grant-maintained schools have experienced to date, rather than an actual increase in the quality of education offered by the school. The existence of a limited number of schools that are funded at a different rate may increase enrolment but does little to affect the basic educational standards in those schools. In fact the opposite might be true in that it can reinforce the *status quo* and increase reluctance to accept change.

Grant-maintained schools as private monopolies

Just as the privatisation of large industries from public to private monopolies does not, in itself, increase productivity, changing from LEA to individual school control does not, of necessity, improve the provision for the consumer of education. Putting more or all the power in the hands of the parents may be a more radical solution than the existing grant-maintained provision. The present situation, with all the power in the hands of the governing body, may be establishing a series of individual monopoly suppliers. The governors, in running the school, may seek to make it exclusive and in doing so not give enough attention to the performance indicators that measure the educational outputs. Their possible lack of understanding and experience of current educational thinking together with their over-zealousness to re-establish perceived traditional standards without due consideration of their relevance to the pupils may result in the creation of an inward-looking school, divorced from the real world. While these exclusive schools may appear attractive to parents, it may be for the wrong reasons. Grant-maintained status is only worthwhile if it results in increased learning outputs that relate to the whole child and the place its pupil will take in society as we approach the twenty-first century.

Autocratic management styles

It was stated earlier that one person's decentralisation is another person's centralisation. Without the moderating effect of the LEA, headteachers of grant-maintained schools can accumulate far more power in their role. Thus staff involvement, participation and commitment can be significantly reduced if headteachers use this increase in power to take more control into their own hands. The AMMA report (Appendix D, pp. 156–64) suggests that this is a possible outcome of grant-maintained status and, certainly, from their survey, no enfranchisement of teachers in terms of more involvement in their professional lives is evident to date.

Governors becoming managers instead of governing

Grant-maintained status means that governors have total control of the school and, as a result, they may attempt to involve themselves more in the day-to-day management of it and try to become more proactive in the organisation of the curriculum and other areas traditionally controlled by the professionals. The effects of this could be disastrous and far worse than the influence and bureaucracy imposed by a (relatively) distant LEA. Not only does it mean that the senior managers in the school are unable to carry out their responsibilities in a productive and fulfilling manner but that the philosophy and attraction of decentralisation is totally lost. Here, once again we come across the danger that one person's decentralisation can become another person's centralisation. If this happens, staff at all levels can receive confused messages about the management of the school which may result in a loss of commitment and motivation.

The role of the governors can be compared with that of the members of the board of a commercial business and that of the headteacher with the managing director. It is vital that governors take on the more strategic role of governing and leave the tactical management of the school to its senior staff. Unfortunately there are examples drawn from the early schools to opt out of exactly the opposite happening and evidence of staff becoming frustrated and demotivated.

Erosion of staff rights

In the past teachers have been protected with regards to their salary, conditions of service and job security by agreements negotiated by their unions at national and LEA level. Grant-maintained status, as well as local management of schools, means that security of tenure has been lost as the practice of redeployment no longer exists. Additionally there are threats to job security and staff rights in this new framework. With the appointment, discipline and dismissal of individual staff in the hands of individual governing bodies, staff no longer have the support of the LEA framework when it comes to dealing with these matters in school. Staff could be subject to the idiosyncratic decisions of governing bodies as has been witnessed in the private sector.

A few grant-maintained schools have refused to recognise unions in their school for negotiating purposes and, while these may be isolated cases, it does suggest a potential and actual threat to staff in these schools. It also demonstrates a difference in perception of the role of the teaching force in a school: hired help or involved professionals?

By contrast a number of schools have set up representative, negotiating committees in their institutions which is encouraging and it is clear that the focus of trade union activity will switch to plant level bargaining in individual schools. How new, local, school-based staff and management relationships develop is a significant area for concern and is addressed in the final chapter when the way in which a school can develop a fully integrated personnel function is considered.

Maintaining rather than developing standards

This relates back to the accountability of grant-maintained schools. The problem is that, without the controlling influence of an LEA, schools may focus on maintaining standards rather than striving to continue to improve them. This is analogous to the principle of quality control rather than quality management. Because the school is oversubscribed and achieving examination results that are comparable with the national average, there may be no incentive to improve the standards set. The school may find itself in a downward spiral that may not become evident until too late.

CONCLUSION

Both this and the previous chapter attempt to articulate an objective assessment of the advantages and disadvantages of grant-maintained status. In both cases it is too early to draw any firm conclusions from the limited experience to date of the schools that have opted out. As far as the disadvantages are concerned they are obviously potentially very serious, but the extent to which they become real will depend on the unfolding political and organisational change that the education system is subjected to in the near future.

Chapter 11

Managing grant-maintained schools in the 1990s

Perhaps the first question that needs to be asked is: 'Why does a school opt for grant-maintained status?' Although individual schools will provide their own rationale, there appears to be no simple answer, either for the schools as a group or indeed, for any one school, as Cecil Knight explains in Chapter 3. However, for many of the early schools to opt out there was one predominant 'reason'. As the AMMA report on their questionnaire survey (Appendix D, pp. 156–64) points out: 'The main reason for seeking grant-maintained status was the fear of closure or re-organisation' (11 (i)). This is increasingly less likely to be the motivating force; at the time of writing (August 1991) only 20 per cent of the approved or up-and-running schools were subject to conflicting section 12 or section 13 proposals. The desire for self-management and the opportunities it brings is increasingly likely to be the dominant motivating force. Cecil Knight states that it was the challenge of self-management that was the motivating force and 'in changing times it was time to change'. What does this change mean in the 1990s?

This chapter initially reflects on some of the components of an effective self-managing school in the 1990s. It then goes on to consider the management perspectives necessary to manage human, financial and physical resources in this new environment. It is only by reassessing and adopting new approaches that the challenge of self-management will be met.

WHAT DOES SELF-MANAGEMENT MEAN?

It is about much more than protecting the selective nature or the single-sex character of the school. Schools thinking of coming out of LEA control have to decide whether they want to be more efficient LEA schools or effective self-managing schools. Do they carry on as before or adopt radical new ways of thinking? They need to consider the allocation of their resources and whether they merely follow an incremental approach which reinforces past patterns or use the opportunity to adopt a zero-based approach. This involves reassessing how they utilise the resources and organise the educational process to achieve enhanced educational outputs.

We suggest self-managing schools should have the following characteristics:

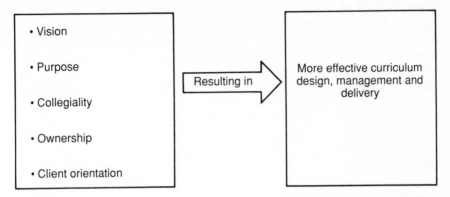

- Vision

- Purpose

- Collegiality

- Ownership

- Client orientation

Resulting in

More effective curriculum design, management and delivery

Vision

A successful grant-maintained school needs a clear vision of where it is going. The school needs to consider its long-term aims and ensure that these are shared and understood by all staff, parents, governors and pupils. This includes consideration of: What are the aims of the school? What sort of school do they want it to be in five years' time? What sort of school will it be? What are the educational values and ethics of the school? How will the partners in the educational process strive to achieve these aims? Having identified them, what are the stages that are necessary to work towards these aims? All these questions and many more need to be considered over a period of time by the governors, staff and parents so that the school does have a definite vision and mission and everyone involved with it is communicating and working towards the same ultimate goals.

It is neither easy nor quick to establish a vision for a school but, as it forms part of the school's development planning process, it is a vital activity. It is important that the governors, staff and parents have a clear understanding of where the school is in every respect and every mode of operation before they begin to develop their vision for the future. This necessarily involves all the partners and provides useful opportunities for building and enhancing relationships and understanding amongst governors, staff and parents. The key feature is the process and the management of this provides one of the significant challenges for grant-maintained schools in the 1990s.

Purpose

An effective self-managing school must have a purpose that is explicit to everyone involved with it and is projected in the message that the school communicates to the external environment. This purpose should reflect the aims and values of the school and be present in the day-to-day work within it.

Collegiality

If the purpose of grant-maintained status is to enhance the teaching and learning within the school then consideration must be given to how the majority of the staff of the school, both teaching and non-teaching, benefit from it and how their contributions may be maximised. It is suggested that governors and senior staff consider a collegial approach as a way of achieving this and demonstrating that the school is using the opportunity for decentralisation to its full extent.

Collegiality can only be achieved through real involvement. All the partners, the staff in particular, need to be given the opportunity to become involved in the planning and development of the school in order to create a sense of ownership. This is possible if governors and senior staff adopt a management approach that is collegial and does involve staff and others, thereby nurturing a sense of ownership.

Ownership

It is reasonable to suggest that the most successful way of improving an individual's output, in whatever form it takes, is to give some ownership of the process or product. This is also true of the partners in the school situation. All those involved and concerned with the school, the pupils, the parents, the staff and the governors, need to be given a sense of ownership of their school, thereby developing a commitment to it. This point is supported by Keith Barker in his conclusion to Chapter 5.

Client orientation

The pupils and the parents are the main clients of the school and the focus of the school's activities should be in meeting their wants and needs. Schools do not exist to provide teaching or office staff with jobs but to provide children with education! It is vital that schools develop and project a culture that recognises the centrality of the clients and does not present the historical school approach whereby the professionals know best and determine needs and wants in isolation from the clients they are serving.

More effective curriculum design, management and delivery

It has already been suggested that the main purpose of grant-maintained status must be about improving the educational outputs of the school in an explicit and measurable way. The establishment of efficient administrative and financial systems is a necessary part of self-management but it is a matter of concern if these are seen as an end in themselves. Grant-maintained schools need to find ways of harnessing these systems to the benefit of the educational outputs as a method of achieving more effective curriculum design, management and delivery. Then they need effective measurements of performance to assess the only significant evaluation factor: has student learning improved?

DEVELOPING RESOURCES TO MEET EDUCATIONAL NEEDS

Having discussed the characteristics of a self-managing school the next key to success for grant-maintained schools is how effectively they manage their resources, human, financial and physical, in order to provide an effective learning environment for their pupils. Chapters 5 and 6 considered the management of financial and physical resources while Chapters 7 and 8 considered the organisation and development of human resources. In all these chapters the authors have described how they have coped with the transition to grant-maintained status. These early schools in the grant-maintained sector are now grappling with the necessity to project their development beyond this initial, transitional phase. In these areas and others, we now pose some of the considerations that should influence these and other schools on their journeys to becoming effective self-managing schools.

Managing human resources

How all of the partners in the school contribute to the effective management of the institution presents one of the key organisational design challenges for grant-maintained schools in the 1990s. They need to consider individual roles in terms of:

- policy approval;
- policy generation;
- policy implementation; and
- policy administration.

Who is involved in each of these activities and how they contribute to each part of the school's planning cycle must be considered and forms the initial philosophical debate that the school managers and governors must address. The school may adopt the public school management approach which can be represented diagrammatically as:

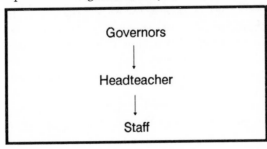

This is the traditional line management model. Alternatively, they may adopt a more collegiate stance with the partnership functioning as below:

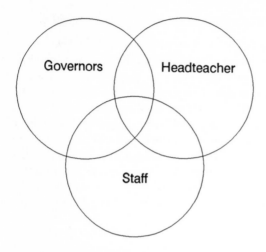

The governors and the headteacher are in the same team and need a method of integrating their efforts while still retaining their specific responsibilities. An interesting perspective on this is provided in Chapter 5 of Davies and Ellison (1990). Governors must be in the business of governing not managing. They provide two functions: first they are responsible for the strategic, long-term view of the school; and second, they act on behalf of the local community by providing an audit of the school in terms of its educational goals and assessing how far it has achieved them. To be in a position to achieve this, the governing body needs to be involved with the staff of the school in designing and operating a school development plan. This sets both the annual targets for the school against which an evaluation of performance can be measured and also provides the longer-term vision and aims for the school. School development planning needs to involve all staff at some stage in the cycle so that there is ownership which will be reflected in the implementation of the policies rather than be perceived as another directive from above.

The way in which the governors and staff work together is the key to the success, or otherwise, of the school; the different contributions of both parties need to be maximised in the interests of the institution. By working together co-operatively and with each person adopting an appropriate and relevant role, the overall result can be considerably more than the sum of the individual parts each person contributes.

A collegiate approach that is based upon genuine delegated responsibility with the appropriate support, provides a way forward for self-managing schools that encourages and enhances involvement and, therefore, commitment from staff at all levels. This approach involves 'flattening out' the hierarchy so that all staff, at whatever level, have responsibility and are part of the overall management structure. This means that, although still predominately role-centred, there is an element of a task-orientated culture.

In order to provide a framework in which teachers can take a significant role in some aspects of school management, there needs to be a well tuned communications system and opportunities for team building. This is likely to involve reviewing the internal structure of the school and the combining of groups so that viable teams are possible. This faculty concept is nothing new but, for it to be successful then there must be well defined and shared values surrounding it.

In addition, each internal group needs to be seen as a management unit with a delegated budget and accompanying responsibilities, thereby creating different opportunities, nurturing new skills and enhancing job satisfaction for staff. This means that the traditional structure of the fairly disjointed academic and pastoral sides of school life should be replaced. All members of staff have pastoral responsibilities which should complement their curriculum roles and ensure that there is integration and unity of approach. Having considered structure, roles and responsibilities, schools need to consider how they manage their staff.

Developing a personnel function in a school

Within the LEA framework, schools have traditionally operated staff development and in-service training policies. However, they have still relied on the LEA for many of the personnel functions that a good employer would provide. This support disappears when a school achieves grant-maintained status and the school must take on total responsibility for managing and developing its staff. The governors and senior staff need to include the following points in their considerations when establishing a school-based personnel policy:

- Establishing a whole school policy, for all staff, including non-teaching staff.
- Integrating policy from job definition, appointment, development, retraining and leaving.
- Defining organisational needs and designing a personnel development policy that meets these needs.
- Integrating appraisal into all aspects of personnel policy.
- Developing empowered professionals and not just employees.
- Relating flexible budgets to flexible staffing and salary structures.
- Implementing performance related pay.
- Implementing succession planning.

In elaborating these points it is worth starting from the basic truth that the most important school resource, apart from pupils, is its staff. The quality and motivation of these people are the responsibility of the school to enhance and develop. The school can no longer blame LEA staffing policies; it is its prime responsibility to deliver effective teaching and promote effective learning.

A policy that takes an employee from appointment to retirement, from induction to retraining, from instruction to professional development is needed. How the staff themselves are involved in determining the policy and designing a programme that is professionally relevant to their needs remains one of the central issues. This can only take place within the organisational context of the school development plan when individual teachers understand their place in the overall scheme and have an opportunity to refine that scheme. It is in this way that a group of empowered professionals can be developed.

However, a whole-school personnel policy may not work because it is all too frequently assumed that a change in the organisational design and management style will automatically bring about the desired changes in individual and organisational behaviour without due regard to any changes in the reward system. This is not necessarily true and consideration needs to be given to what behaviour is required to be achieved. For example, possible objectives may include:

- motivation of performance.
- motivation of personal development.
- attraction and retention of certain individuals.
- establishment of required culture.
- establishment of required structures.
- establishment of certain costs.

The desired changes need to be approached in the following order:

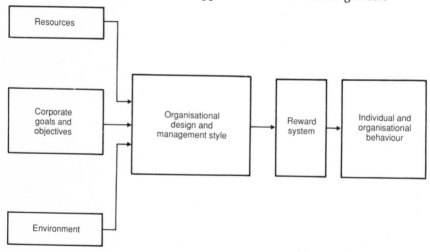

Staff development and appraisal, although key to this way of considering staff in school, are in fact just part of the broader concept of personnel management. The concept of treating people as individuals and empowering them to have more control over their working lives also begs the question of rewarding staff. If there are flexible budgets in terms of choice of resource expenditure is it desirable to reward every teacher on the same salary despite the different contributions they make? Performance related pay may be the way to achieve and reward excellence in schools (see Tomlinson, 1992). It needs to be linked into the decentralisation within the school so that the individual understands and is involved in the management issues. Additionally, it needs to acknowledge skills and competencies over and above those described in a job description.

Higher salaries by negotiation should not just be the prerogative of headteachers; that would just be centralisation at another level. If salaries motivate and enhance performance then others, as well as headteachers, should have their motivation and performance enhanced. In fact, headteachers negotiating salary increases for themselves in isolation from their staff is an unfortunate example for staff. From a governor's perspective, there is nothing wrong with increasing the salary of headteachers by 25 per cent as long as they can increase their output, as measured by appropriate performance indicators previously agreed with the governors, also by 25 per cent. This concept of performance related pay is long overdue in education.

Managing financial resources

Amongst the early problems that every grant-maintained school must face is the need to come to grips with the new administration of finances and the use of the appropriate computer package to run the school-based operation. Taking over the budget operated previously by the LEA presents a whole new set of responsibilities for the school. Initial emphasis concerns the appointment of an administrator or bursar and the establishment of appropriate administrative systems. As Roger Perks points out in Chapter 4, it is important that the headteacher and senior management, as well as the governors, do not become immersed in the day-to-day administration of the budget and, in so doing, they neglect to develop a resource management perspective.

This last perspective can best be considered in two ways: that of the budgetary cycle and of the elements of the budgetary process. The budgeting cycle consists of the following four stages:

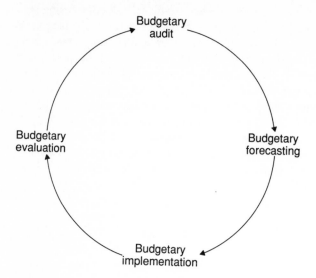

The significance from a management perspective of looking forward is to avoid a reactive response to having to prepare the budget, implement it and ensure that the mechanics of 'doing the budget' become part of the much broader cycle. These stages should form part of the much wider organisational planning cycle and can briefly be explained as follows.

Budgetary audit

The school needs to consider where the organisation is now and what its curricular, staffing, material and other needs and priorities are. Unless the school carries out an audit of all its activities, it will be assessing finance out of context. Finance is the facilitator of the educational process and should not be seen in isolation. Unlike in a business situation, profit is not the ultimate evaluator – effective education is. Therefore, having a clear understanding of the identified educational goals and consequent resource needs should be the first priority of the school managers. However, one of the dangers of finance committees in schools is that they make decisions based purely on the figures placed in front of them on the balance sheets and do not take into account the relevant educational effects of such decisions.

Budgetary forecasting

Making financial decisions on a one-year perspective only means that the school is making these decisions in isolation from their impact. For example, consider a secondary school which finds itself overspent by £20,000. This is not very significant if the school is experiencing an increase in its applications and subsequent numbers-on-roll for the next academic year because there will be a corresponding increase in its formula funded budget. Conversely, an overspend with a declining pupil base and a consequent fall in resources, presents a much more serious problem. Thus it is important that, as a key element of the budgetary process, the school attempts to forecast its future income and expenditure trends.

Similarly, on the expenditure side, appointing a teacher at the bottom of the salary scale compared to one at the top can involve a difference in salary cost of as much as £6,000. Considered over five years, even as the cheaper teacher begins to move up the scale, the difference is in the region of £25,000. Additionally, trends are identifiable if expenditure on renewable materials or replacing computer equipment are projected over a number of years. Therefore, one of the key elements in the budgetary process is assessing income and expenditure flows over a period of time so that individual budget decisions for a particular year can be set in context.

Budgetary implementation

All schools are used to being involved in this process. It is important that governors and staff of the school see the financial decisions not in isolation, but as part of the cycle, following on after the first two stages of auditing and forecasting have been completed. It is also worth considering how the budgetary process is undertaken, who is involved and how teachers contribute to the process, so that staff regard the budget as a financial expression of the educational goals of the school and not as a secretive plot by senior staff to exploit them.

Budgetary evaluation

Finally the school should monitor the budget as it is implemented. This is usually something that schools do relatively well in terms of checking whether expenditure is on target, but less well in terms of evaluation. Questions need to be asked and answers attempted in some difficult areas:

- Did the expenditure on those resources result in improved teaching and learning?
- Does employing two classroom assistants instead of one extra teacher give a better learning outcome?

These four stages demonstrate that, in a self-managing school, instead of the budget being considered as a mechanical financial tool, it is vital that it is seen as the key planning instrument in the school's decision-making process. In the 1990s, schools have to develop a resource management perspective of the budgetary process and not just focus on balancing the books once a year.

In the budgetary cycle, each stage involves consideration of the elements in the budgetary process. These traditionally have been concerned with acquisition of resources, the allocation of them once received, actually spending the money and controlling the processes to ensure correct financial procedures. Within the LEA framework these four stages have been largely predetermined by the authority, with the school having limited discretion over the operational processes. However, schools have had no control previously over the strategic elements in the process: those of planning educational income and expenditure, choosing between different resource combinations, and evaluating whether those choices have enhanced the teaching and learning process. While a school is grappling with the process of taking over the operational elements from the LEA, it also needs to ensure that the senior management team develops the skills to undertake successfully the strategic management activities of planning, choice and evaluation. Self-managing schools need therefore to move away from the initial bookkeeping task of implementing an annual budget and set up a budgetary planning cycle with a clear understanding of the necessary elements in the process. Only then will the school start using its budget to further the long-term educational needs of the school and not just be overwhelmed by the administration and mechanics of the task. The challenge for them in the 1990s is to make finance facilitate the educational process and not vice versa.

Managing physical resources: capital development

As with the planning and management of other aspects of grant-maintained schools, property-related issues benefit from a structured approach which adequately reflects the educational needs of the school. It is essential that once the educational objectives have been decided by the school, then they should be translated into property requirements in the form of a strategic development plan.

This plan needs to contain integrated policies which cover both capital development and the planned maintenance of the building stock. The first task for schools must be to set up a decision-making structure that links the governors, the headteacher and the staff for the purpose of analysis and decisions about school development planning and subsequent property-related decisions. Also in its external relationships a single point of contact is advisable between the school and the professional advisers to ensure clear and unambiguous decision-making at all stages.

It is important to emphasise the increased responsibilities relating to property which fall entirely within the jurisdiction of the school governors on achieving grant-maintained status. Under LEA control all major property matters were dealt with at arms length by the local authority staff. In many ways the basic problem of lack of finance for capital development and planned maintenance still exists under grant-maintained status. However, this is now no longer someone else's problem, for the responsibility lies firmly with the governors of grant-maintained schools for the care, maintenance and development of the school's facilities. Against this challenging background, the schools which adopt a carefully thought out and structured approach to the problems associated with their new status benefit from the greater opportunities for success within the system.

Development planning

The importance of school development planning has been emphasised within this book and includes capital development planning. For example, the number and function of teaching spaces required will depend on both the subjects taught and timetabling. This in turn affects staffing levels and associated costs together with future staffing policies. In essence, this development plan should:

- translate educational targets into property requirements;
- assess the existing building facilities;
- compare the current provision with the DES statutory requirements;
- assess the site potential including physical and planning constraints to development;
- consider the logistics of operating a school during future developments;
- identify the key areas of building maintenance and energy conservation which may be relevant to future planning; and
- produce an integrated development plan showing a logical progression from the point of incorporation to the attainment of the long-term objectives.

Having established these key factors the following need to be considered when they are put into action:

- compliance with the Education (School Premises) Regulations 1981;
- funding limits within the grant-maintained sector;
- requirements for planned maintenance;
- current educational requirements, for example, implementation of the National Curriculum;
- opportunities for energy conservation;
- compliance with all relevant design guidelines and legislation affecting construction works.

It is, therefore, vital for a school to consider educational objectives, school development planning, capital development, maintenance planning, energy conservation and financial planning as closely linked issues. By adopting a structured and co-ordinated approach to the integration of the various facets of managing the physical resources in a grant-maintained school the benefits can be measured in terms of improved learning outcomes.

CONCLUSION

> Educational improvements have not been an early priority – the few dramatic modifications suggest that they could have been.
>
> AMMA report (see Appendix D, para 55)

The ultimate evaluation of self-managing schools is provided in the answers to the questions: Do the children benefit? Is the teaching and learning process enhanced and improved to give greater educational outputs? This can be expressed diagrammatically as follows:

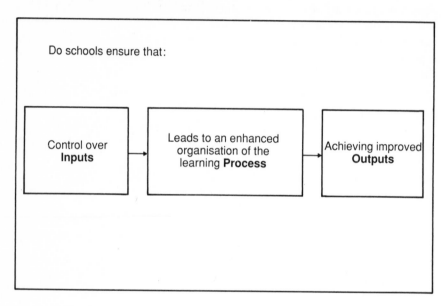

As Roger Perks points out in Chapter 4 grant-maintained status does not in itself guarantee enhanced educational outputs. The organisational decentralisation from LEA to school level can merely replace one bureaucracy with another. The AMMA report (see Appendix D, para 52) provides a significant comment on this:

> LEA bureaucracy and inefficiency is not the only form of bureaucracy and inefficiency. The polarisation of the administrative and educational aims of a school is a genuine irritation to teachers, as is school bureaucracy and financial mismanagement.

What grant-maintained status has to offer is the opportunity for decentralisation within the school so that it becomes empowering for teachers, parents and students. It should enable them to take more control and gain more involvement in the educational process. Greater involvement and ownership of the educational process leads to increased satisfaction within the school resulting in improved teaching and learning and thus increased educational outputs.

In the first chapter it was suggested that the three criteria on which to examine self-managing schools, and grant-maintained schools in particular, were increased flexibility, productivity and accountability. The evidence from the contributors to this book would suggest that they have made considerable use of the flexibility to deploy resources in ways which they perceive will enhance the organisational and educational process in their schools. Critics of grant-maintained schools would argue that the enhanced level of resources makes flexibility more possible. However, it is not just the level of resources that has given this flexibility but it is the creative freedom of self-management that has enabled grant-maintained schools to be more flexible in their management of resources. Whether this has led to increased educational productivity is yet to be seen. This remains the challenge for grant-maintained schools. To be fair, it is obviously too early to evaluate whether different management decisions have led to increased outputs, although it may be a significant consideration for governors when salaries are being negotiated. As to accountability, market accountability in the form of increased applications suggests that the clients are receiving a product they want. Whether in the long-term this is an adequate replacement for the removal of democratically elected local control remains to be seen.

The challenge remains for grant-maintained schools to improve significantly the quality of education of the children in their care. We hope this book will stimulate the appropriate debate so that, whatever the political developments, improved educational performance remains at the centre of the movement towards self-managing schools.

REFERENCE

Davies, B. and Ellison, L. (1990) *Managing the Primary School Budget*, London: Northcote House.
Tomlinson, H. (1992) *Performance-related Pay in Education*, London: Routledge.

Part IV

Appendices

Appendix A

A review of opting out to date – number of schools (at 31 August 1991)

SCHOOLS THAT HAVE BEEN APPROVED FOR GRANT-MAINTAINED STATUS AS OF 31 AUGUST 1991 (BY FORMER LEA)

Inner London Boroughs

Cardinal Vaughan Memorial School	Kensington
Claremont GM High School	Brent
Graveney School	Wandsworth
London Nautical School	Southwark
London Oratory School	Hammersmith
Raines Foundation School	Tower Hamlets

Greater London

Bishopshalt School	Hillingdon
Bullers Wood School for Girls	Bromley
Coopers School	Bromley
Greenway School	Hillingdon
Haydon School	Hillingdon
Hayes School	Bromley
Hendon School	Barnet
Highams Park School	Waltham Forest
Langley Park Boys School	Bromley
Nonsuch High School For Girls	Sutton
Queen Elizabeth's Boys School	Barnet
Queensmead School	Hillingdon
Stratford GM School	Newham
Vyners School	Hillingdon
Wilsons School	Sutton

Greater Manchester

Audenshaw High School	Tameside
St James' C of E School	Bolton

Merseyside

St Francis Xavier's College	Liverpool

West Midlands

Baverstock GM School	Birmingham
Great Barr GM School	Birmingham
Handsworth Grammar School	Birmingham

Manor High School	Sandwell
Moseley Park School	Wolverhampton
Old Swinford Hospital	Dudley
Small Heath School	Birmingham
Wolverhampton Girls High School	Wolverhampton

West Yorkshire

Bingley Grammar School	Bradford
Castle Hall GM School	Kirklees
The Crossley Heath School	Calderdale
Heckmondwike Grammar School	Kirklees
North Halifax High School	Calderdale

Counties

Beechen Cliff School	Avon
Oldfield School	
Queensbury School	Bedfordshire
Reading School	Berkshire
St Bartholomew's School	
Southlands School	
Beaconsfield High School	Buckinghamshire
Bridgewater Hall School	
Brindley Hall School	
St Helen's Primary School	Cambridgeshire
The Bankfield School	Cheshire
Kirbie Kendal School	Cumbria
Ecclesbourne School	Derbyshire
Netherthorpe School	
Colyton Grammar School	Devon
Bournemouth School	Dorset
The Woodroffe School	
Chalvedon School	Essex
Westcliff High School for Boys	
Marling School	Gloucestershire
Pates Grammar School	
Ribston Hall High School	
Stroud High School	
The Arnewood School	Hampshire
The Burgate School	
Hardley School	
Francis Bacon School	Hertfordshire
Parmiters School	
Rickmansworth School	
St Mary's RC Primary School	
Watford Girls Grammar School	
Watford Grammar School	
Wold Newton Primary School	Humberside

The Cornwallis School	Kent
Dartford Grammar School	
The Grammar School for Girls, Wilmington	
Homewood School	
Maplesden Noakes School	
St George's C of E School	
Southlands School	
Thamesview School	
Wilmington Grammar School for Boys	
Bacup and Rawtenstall Grammar School	Lancashire
Clitheroe Royal Grammar School	
Lancaster Girls Grammar School	
Lancaster Royal Grammar School	
Newton C of E School	
Long Field High School	Leicestershire
Bourne Abbey Primary School	Lincolnshire
Caistor Grammar School	
Carres Grammar School	
King Edward VI School	
Kings School	
Queen Elizabeth's Grammar School	
St George's School	
Skegness Grammar School	
Wainfleet Magdalen C of E/Methodist	
Heacham Middle School	Norfolk
Wymondham College	
Kingsley Park GM Middle School	Northamptonshire
Kingswood School	
Moulton Primary School	
Southfield School for Girls	
Adams Grammar School	Shropshire
Sexeys School	Somerset
Collingwood GM School	Surrey
Guildford County School	
St John the Baptist School	
Avon Valley School	Warwickshire
Exhall School	
St Augustine's RC Comprehensive	Wiltshire

Wales

Cwmcarn GM Comprehensive School	Gwent

MINDED TO APPROVE

Greater London

Ravens Wood School for Boys	Bromley

Greater Manchester

Crossgates Primary School	Rochdale

Counties
　　Redgate Middle School   Norfolk

'YES' VOTES, PROPOSALS PUBLISHED, AWAITING THE DECISION OF THE SECRETARY OF STATE

Inner London Boroughs
　　Burntwood School   Wandsworth
　　La Retraite School   Lambeth

Greater London
　　Barnhill Comprehensive School   Hillingdon
　　Brentside High School   Ealing
　　Copland Community School   Brent
　　Crofton Junior School   Bromley
　　Drayton Manor High School   Ealing
　　Ellen Wilkinson School   Ealing
　　Greenford High School   Ealing
　　Hayes Manor School   Hillingdon
　　John Fisher School   Sutton
　　Kelsey Park School   Bromley
　　Mellow Lane School   Hillingdon
　　Northolt High School   Ealing
　　Northwood School   Hillingdon
　　Riddlesdown High School   Croydon
　　Townmead School   Hillingdon
　　Walford High School   Ealing
　　William Gladstone School   Brent
　　Wood End First School   Ealing
　　Wood End Middle School   Ealing

West Yorkshire
　　Salterlee Junior and Infant School   Calderdale
　　Woolley C of E First School   Wakefield

Counties
　　Desborough Comprehensive School   Berkshire

　　Gamlingay Village College (Middle)   Cambridgeshire
　　Newborough Primary School

　　Arley Primary School   Cheshire
　　Kettleshulme C of E Primary School

　　Bowness-on-Solway Primary School   Cumbria
　　Eden School
　　Queen Elizabeth School
　　St Aidan's School

　　Budmouth School   Dorset

　　Elmbridge School   Essex
　　Elmwood County Primary School
　　King John School
　　The Park School, Rayleigh
　　The Philip Morant School
　　The Plume School

The Crypt School	Gloucestershire
Ringwood Comprehensive School	Hampshire
Christ Church C of E JMI School	Hertfordshire
Appledore C of E Primary School	Kent
Aylsford School	
Cliffe Woods Middle School	
Dartford Grammar School for Girls	
Edenbridge Middle School	
Oakwood Park Grammar School	
Senacre High School	
Sheppey School	
Simon Langton Boys Grammar School	
Snodland C of E Primary School	
Wrotham School	
Yarborough High School	Lincolnshire
King John Middle School	Northamptonshire
Northampton School for Boys	
De Stafford School	Surrey
Glyn School	
Gordons School	
Manor County First School	
Hawkedale First School	
Heathside Secondary School	
Send C of E First School	
Hartshill School	Warwickshire

Wales

Bishop Vaughn RC Comprehensive School	West Glamorgan
Bryn Mawr School	Gwent
Cefn Pennar	

'YES' VOTE, GOVERNORS' PROPOSALS TO THE SECRETARY OF STATE

Inner London Boroughs

Ethelburga JMI School	Wandsworth
Turnham Junior School	Lewisham

Greater London

Cheam High School	Sutton
Beaverbrook School for Girls	Bromley
Newstead Wood School	Bromley

South Yorkshire

Wortly C of E Junior and Infant School	Barnsley

West Midlands

Hatchford Junior and Infant School	Solihull

Counties

Deanefield School	Berkshire
Langley Grammar School	

Brookmead First and Middle School	Buckinghamshire
Hassall Green Methodist Primary	Cheshire
Boyton County Primary School	Cornwall
Hayton C of E Primary School	Cumbria
Belmont Primary School Borrow Wood Junior School	Derbyshire
Parkstone Grammar School	Dorset
Newlands Spring County Primary	Essex
Parkside First School	Hertfordshire
Cliffe Woods Primary School Cranbrook School Fulston Manor School Oldborough Manor High School Rainham Mark Grammar School The Skinners School	Kent
Baines School	Lancashire
Castle Hills School Gartree School Lincoln Christ's Hospital School North Rauceby School William Alvey Junior School	Lincolnshire
The Admiral's Middle School Downham Market High School Dereham Church First School Gresham Primary School Loddon Middle School Norwich Road First School	Norfolk
Bliss Charity Primary School Lodge Park School	Northamptonshire
Ravensdale Middle School	Nottinghamshire
Blindley Heath C of E First School Epsom and Ewell High School South Holmwood C of E First School Stoneleigh First School	Surrey
Myton School	Warwickshire

BALLOT PENDING

Inner London Boroughs
Huntingfield Primary School — Wandsworth

West Midlands
Darlaston Community School — Walsall

West Yorkshire
Deighton High School — Kirklees

Counties

Thomas Whitehead Church Lower School	Bedfordshire
Queen Catherine School	Cumbria
Hamilton County Primary School	Essex
Robinswood Primary School	Gloucestershire
Monksmead First School	Hertfordshire
Angley School	Kent
Brockhill Park School	
Ormskirk Grammar School	Lancashire
Cromer High School	Norfolk
Lyne and Long Cross C of E First School	Surrey
Rokeby Middle School	Warwickshire

PROPOSALS REJECTED BY THE SECRETARY OF STATE AFTER A SUCCESSFUL BALLOT

Inner London Boroughs

Harwood School	Hammersmith
Walsingham School	Wandsworth

Greater London

Ramsden School for Girls	Bromley

Greater Manchester

Hindley Park High School	Wigan

West Midlands

The Longlands School	Dudley
Simon Digby Comprehensive School	Solihull

Counties

Fosters Boys Grammar School	Dorset
Lord Digby's Girls Grammar School	
Highwood School	Gloucestershire
Sir James Altham School	Hertfordshire
Castlemount School	Kent
Swanscombe High School	
Blessed Hugh More RC Secondary School	Lincolnshire
Southpark High School	
Kettering Boys School	Northamptonshire
The Down Primary School	Shropshire
Ellerdine Primary School	

Wales

Queens School, Newport	Gwent

'NO' VOTE

Inner London Boroughs
Chestnut Grove School	Wandsworth
St Theresa's RC Secondary Girls School	Lewisham

Greater London
Featherstone High School	Ealing
Gaynes School	Havering
Nower Hill High School	Harrow
Preston Manor High School	Brent
St Paul's C of E Primary School	Barnet
Villiers High School	Ealing
Woodford County High School	Redbridge
Ravensbourne School for Girls	Bromley

Greater Manchester
Droylsden County High School	Tameside
Failsworth Upper School	Oldham
Queen Elizabeth's Senior High School	Rochdale
Sale Grammar School for Boys	Trafford
Siddal Moor High School	Rochdale

Merseyside
Ruffwood School	Knowsley

South Yorkshire
Armthorpe Comprehensive School	Doncaster
Dearneside Comprehensive School	Barnsley
Silverdale School	Sheffield

Tyne and Wear
Whickham School	Gateshead

West Midlands
Alexandra High School	Sandwell
Grange School	Dudley
Sir Wilfred Martineau School	Birmingham
Tudor Grange School	Solihull
Underhill Junior School	Wolverhampton

West Yorkshire
Boothroyd Junior School	Kirklees

Counties
Ailwyn Community School	Cambridgeshire
St Gregory's RC High School	Cheshire
St Joseph's RC High School	
Weaverham High School	
Wade Deacon County School	
Chesterfield School	Derbyshire
Eckington School	
St Helena School	
Silverhill Primary School	
Warmbrook Junior School	
King Edward VI School	Devon

Bridport County Primary School	Dorset
King James First Comprehensive School	Durham
Sir Thomas Richs School	Gloucestershire
Blackfield Middle School Kings School South Farnborough County Infants School	Hampshire
Queen Elizabeth High School	Hereford and Worcester
Hadham Hall School John Henry Newman School	Hertfordshire
Waltham Toll Bar School	Humberside
Hoo St Werburgh Middle School St Peter's Primary School Weald of Kent Grammar School	Kent
Blackpool Sixth Form College Morecambe High School	Lancashire
Manor High School	Leicestershire
Ripon Grammar School Romanby County Primary School	North Yorkshire
Bishop Stopford School Blackthorn Middle School Booth Lower School Chichele School	Northamptonshire
High Oakham Middle School Windmill Ridge School	Nottinghamshire
Banbury School	Oxfordshire
Neroche Primary School	Somerset
St Thomas More RC High School	Staffordshire
Westfield County First School	Surrey
Millais School	West Sussex
Ridgeway School	Wiltshire

Wales

John Beddoes School	Powys
Olchfa School West	Glamorgan
Ysgol Emrys ap Iwan	Clwyd

Scotland

Willowbank Primary School	Glasgow

A review of opting out to date – analysis of schools (at 31 August 1991)

OVERVIEW

At present there are 109 schools either operating as GM or approved but not yet open. Of these schools 6 are from the Inner London boroughs, 15 from Greater London, 2 from Greater Manchester, 1 from Mersyside, 8 from the West Midlands, 5 from West Yorkshire, 71 from the English counties and 1 from Wales. The following analysis appertains to all 109 schools.

Type	Primary	:	7 schools	(6%)
	Middle	:	3 schools	(3%)
	High	:	1 school	(1%)
	Secondary	:	98 schools	(90%)
Secondary age range				
	11–18	:	73 schools	(75%)
	12–18	:	6 schools	(6%)
	13–18	:	2 schools	(2%)
	14–18	:	1 school	(1%)
	11–16	:	13 schools	(13%)
	12–16	:	3 schools	(3%)
Secondary character				
	Comprehensive	:	64 schools	(65%)
	Selective	:	34 schools	(35%)
	Boarding	:	11 schools	(11%)
Sex	Girls	:	11 schools	(10%)
	Boys	:	22 schools	(20%)
	Mixed	:	76 schools	(70%)
Ex-status	VA	:	11 schools	(10%)
	VC	:	13 schools	(12%)
	C of E	:	2 schools	(2%)
	RC	:	3 schools	(3%)
	Methodist	:	1 school (joint)	(1%)

ANALYSIS BY FORMER LEA

Inner London Boroughs

Type	Secondary	:	6 schools	(100%)
Secondary age range				
	11–18	:	6 schools	(100%)
Secondary character				
	Comprehensive	:	5 schools	(83%)
	Selective	:	1 school	(17%)
Sex	Boys	:	3 schools	(50%)
	Mixed	:	3 schools	(50%)
			5 schools are mixed at sixth form level	
Ex-status	VA	:	2 schools	(33%)

Numbers on roll range from 402 to 1,500.

Greater London

Type	Secondary	:	15 schools	(100%)
Secondary age range				
	11–18	:	14 schools	(93%)
	11–16	:	1 school	(7%)
Secondary character				
	Comprehensive	:	13 schools	(87%)
	Selective	:	2 schools	(13%)
Sex	Girls	:	2 schools	(13%)
	Boys	:	3 schools	(20%)
	Mixed	:	10 schools	(67%)

Numbers on roll range from 730 to 1,200.

Greater Manchester

Type	Secondary	:	2 schools	(100%)
Secondary age range				
	11–16	:	2 schools	(100%)
Secondary character				
	Comprehensive	:	2 schools	(100%)
Sex	Boys	:	1 school	(50%)
	Mixed	:	1 school	(50%)

Numbers on roll range from 720 to 748.

Merseyside

Type	Secondary	:	1 school	(100%)
Secondary age range				
	11–18	:	1 school	(100%)
Secondary character				
	Comprehensive	:	1 school	(100%)
Sex	Boys	:	1 school	(100%)

Number on roll is 1,030.

West Midlands

Type	Secondary	:	8 schools	(100%)
Secondary age range				
	11–18	:	5 schools	(63%)
	11–16	:	3 schools	(37%)
Secondary character				
	Comprehensive	:	6 schools	(75%)
	Selective	:	2 schools	(25%)
	Boarding	:	1 school	(11%)
Sex	Girls	:	1 school	(13%)
	Boys	:	2 schools	(25%)
	Mixed	:	5 schools	(62%)
Ex-status	VA	:	1 school	(13%)
	RC	:	1 school	(13%)

Numbers on roll range from 550 to 2,011.

West Yorkshire

Type	Middle	:	1 school	(20%)
	Secondary	:	4 schools	(80%)
Secondary age range				
	11–18	:	3 schools	(75%)
	13–18	:	1 school	(25%)
Secondary character				
	Selective	:	4 schools	(100%)
Sex	Mixed	:	5 schools	(100%)
Ex-status	VA	:	1 school	(20%)
	VC	:	1 school	(20%)

Numbers on roll range from 435 to 940.

Counties

Type	Primary	:	7 schools	(10%)
	Middle	:	2 schools	(3%)
	High	:	1 school	(1%)
	Secondary	:	61 schools	(86%)
Secondary age range				
	11–18	:	44 schools	(72%)
	12–18	:	6 schools	(10%)
	13–18	:	1 school	(2%)
	14–18	:	1 school	(2%)
	11–16	:	6 schools	(10%)
	12–16	:	3 schools	(5%)
Secondary character				
	Comprehensive	:	36 schools	(59%)
	Selective	:	25 schools	(41%)
	Boarding	:	10 schools	(16%)
Sex	Girls	:	8 schools	(11%)
	Boys	:	12 schools	(17%)
	Mixed	:	51 schools	(72%)

Ex-status	VA	:	7 schools	(10%)
	VC	:	12 schools	(17%)
	C of E	:	2 schools	(3%)
	RC	:	2 schools	(3%)
	Methodist	:	1 school (joint)	(1%)

Numbers on roll range from 90 (Primary) to 1,508.

Wales

Type	Secondary	:	1 school	(100%)
Secondary age range				
	11–16	:	1 school	(100%)
Secondary character				
	Comprehensive	:	1 school	(100%)
Sex	Mixed	:	1 school	(100%)

Number on roll is 327.

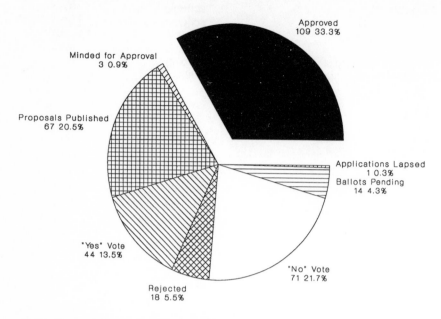

Applications status: summary of position
Note: Total schools to 31 August 1991 is 327

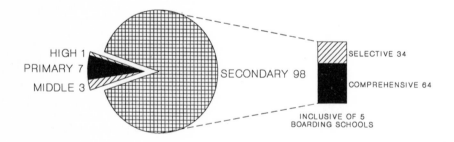

Grant-maintained schools by character
Note: Total schools to 31 August 1991 is 109 (Bar indicates secondary intake)

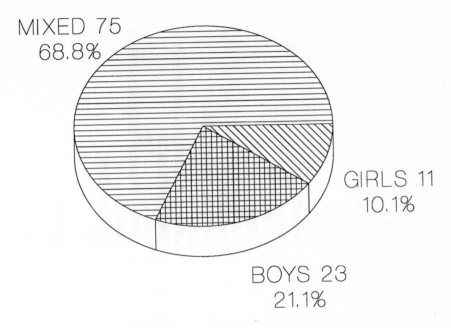

Types of grant-maintained schools (Boys, girls, mixed)
Note: Total schools to 31 August 1991 is 109

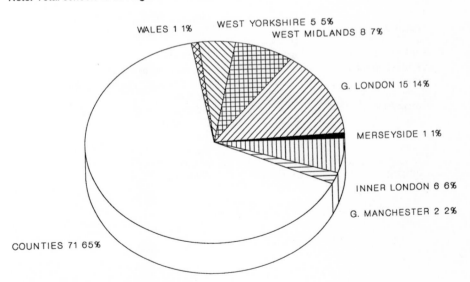

Grant-maintained regional statistics
Note: Total schools to 31 August 1991 is 109

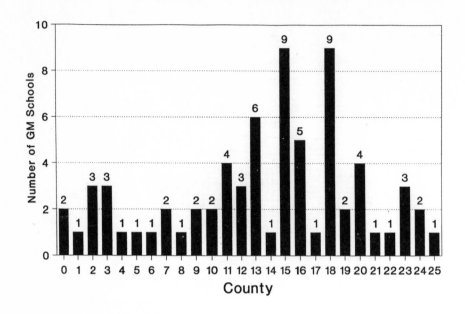

English county distribution, 31 August 1991
Note: Total schools to 31 August 1991 is 71

Key:

County	No.	County	No.
Avon	0	Hertfordshire	13
Bedfordshire	1	Humberside	14
Berkshire	2	Kent	15
Buckinghamshire	3	Lancashire	16
Cambridgeshire	4	Leicestershire	17
Cheshire	5	Lincolnshire	18
Cumbria	6	Norfolk	19
Derbyshire	7	Northamptonshire	20
Devon	8	Shropshire	21
Dorset	9	Somerset	22
Essex	10	Surrey	23
Gloucestershire	11	Warwickshire	24
Hampshire	12	Wiltshire	25

Appendix C

Grant-Maintained Schools – Quality Assurance
A Voluntary Code of Practice

INTRODUCTION

The first generation of grant-maintained schools opened in September 1989. Whilst being motivated by a desire for greater freedom and financial autonomy, staff, governors and parents are deeply committed to raising standards of educational achievement. This code of practice is a manifestation of that commitment.

Governing bodies of grant-maintained schools are invited to subscribe to this Code of Practice and to publish their commitment to it in their school prospectus. The Code itself enables each individual governing body to maintain its own autonomy while establishing the principle that the sector as a whole places high priority on the public demonstration of quality assurance to its clients and to the wider community.

The Code of Practice encompasses a threefold approach:

a internal evaluation.
b HMI inspections.
c other external evaluations.

The governors of grant-maintained schools subscribing to the voluntary code of practice agree to:

1 Publish their own policy statement for quality assurance based upon this code of Practice (see note (a) below).
2 Engage in a continuous process of internal evaluation of the work of the school (see note (b) below).
3 Engage in a planned cycle of external evaluation by impeccable and independent outside bodies. This cycle will ensure that every aspect of the school's work is subject to systematic scrutiny (see notes (c), (d) and (e) below).
4 Publish their commitment to the Code of Practice in their school prospectus.
5 Publish a summary of external evaluations and actions consequent upon them in their annual report to parents (see note (f) below).
6 Register with an independent agency, for example, The Grant-Maintained Schools' Foundation, the fact and date of each external evaluation, the identity of the evaluators and a summary of the report and response which appears in the annual report. This register will be available for public scrutiny.

Notes to the above

a Governors' policy statements may include details of: (i) a mechanism for ensuring that staff have a right of response/comment on any reports made by evaluators; and

(ii) a procedure to ensure that action resulting from evaluation is recorded as part of the process.

b Internal evaluation is an important and necessary part of the process of quality control. Schools would identify their aims and also the evaluation criteria against which they will judge the quality of the work of the whole institution.

c Governors will retain the right to vary the plan at any time, determine a cycle appropriate to their particular school and its curriculum. The cycle would normally be between two and five years.

d Governors, after consulting senior staff, will send to the Heads and Governors Standing Committee of the Foundation a brief report on the quality of the work of their evaluators. The Foundation will then establish a list of accredited evaluators. This list will be made available to subscribing schools. There will be no compulsion to use only those named on it.

e Whilst it will be for individual governing bodies to determine the headings under which external assessors will report, they are likely to include:

- staffing and staff support.
- facilities.
- teaching resources.
- organisation of pupils' work.
- teaching strategies.
- pupil response.
- organisation of internal assessment and evaluation.
- assessment of performance against external criteria (e.g., National Curriculum).
- buildings, plant.
- management strategies.

The governing body will usually wish to identify and make available, in consultation with the external evaluator, appropriate performance indicators for each aspect of the evaluation.

f The publication of the full text of evaluators' reports and action taken as a consequence of them is left to the discretion of individual governing bodies.

Appendix D

The experience of going grant-maintained: the perceptions of AMMA teacher representatives

Report of a questionnaire survey, June 1991 (Summary and conclusions)

BACKGROUND

1 Grant-maintained schools are now the everyday working experience for hundreds of teachers, including AMMA members. While the Education Reform Bill was going through parliament AMMA expressed grave concern about the principle of permitting or encouraging schools to opt out of local authority control. We stated that the government had not established a case for grant-maintained schools and that they would destabilise efforts to maintain an effective, publicly-funded education system. We did not consider that the fragmentation of the education system would necessarily lead to improved standards through competition. We were particularly concerned that the isolation of members in grant-maintained schools could lead to a deterioration in the employment conditions of our members.

2 In April 1989, AMMA published *Grant-Maintained Schools: Advice to AMMA Members*. We stated 'Now that grant-maintained schools are a reality we do not assume that the proposals for opting out necessarily represent salvation or disaster. We will endeavour to represent members' best interests, whether they are personally in favour of a particular proposal or deeply opposed to it.

3 AMMA does not take a partisan stance: members need pragmatic and realistic advice, geared to the particular circumstances of their own school and others in the area. We aim to help members promote their professional well-being and protect their conditions of service in a constructive and practical way.

4 In July 1990, AMMA held a conference for its representatives in grant-maintained schools and it became clear that their experiences were diverse and also that there was considerable interest in trying to get some overall picture of what exactly it meant to go grant-maintained. The association, therefore, decided to send a questionnaire on 'The experience of going grant-maintained' to all its representatives in schools incorporated as grant-maintained schools as of 1 April 1991.

THE SURVEY

5 The questionnaire sought information on the background reasons for going grant-maintained, changes in the management and the management styles of the schools, the morale of the teachers, any changes to conditions of service and working conditions, changes in the professional development opportunities of teachers, and the extent of union recognition. It also allowed AMMA representatives the opportunity to respond in an open-ended way on their views of the experience of going grant-maintained. In order to encourage the highest

possible response rate representatives were assured of confidentiality and anonymity and were offered the opportunity to choose to respond 'don't know' if the representative felt more comfortable with this than pursuing management for information. We were also conscious that we were asking representatives to respond in a very short time scale at a time of the year when many secondary school teachers are intensely busy with public examination responsibilities. In the event, a very s nall minority exercised this option.

THE SAMPLE AND ITS LIMITATIONS

6 The response was extremely gratifying. Of the 62 questionnaires distributed 37 have so far been returned, representing 38 schools, for these purposes the Brindley and Bridgewater schools on the Stantonbury site at Milton Keynes counting as a single school. The breakdown is as follows:

37 questionnaires from:

23 comprehensive and 14 selective schools;

36 secondary schools – of which 27 are 11–18 schools – and one middle school;

22 co-educational schools, 10 boys' schools and 5 girls' schools;

6 of the co-educational schools, 6 boys' schools and 2 girls' schools are selective schools;

16 co-educational, including the middle school, 4 boys' schools and 3 girls' schools are comprehensive schools.

7 By September 1991, 27 of the schools will have been operating as grant-maintained schools for at least a year, a further 4 are now in their second term as a grant-maintained school and 6 have only been incorporated since 1 April 1991.

8 Before proceeding with a preliminary analysis it is perhaps appropriate to make it clear what this survey can not be. It is not an exact survey of the position in grant-maintained schools. It is a survey based on the knowledge and perceptions of AMMA representatives in the schools. That knowledge is not always comprehensive is witnessed by the one questionnaire where a headteacher adds additional, and unsurprisingly, more informed, comments. However, it is perhaps unlikely that a teacher choosing to be identified as a union representative in a school and taking the trouble to complete and return a questionnaire, would be less well informed than the average. These representatives are AMMA's most active members in grant-maintained schools and the members through whom we are alerted to problems and concerns in the schools and on whom we rely to disseminate information and to take preventive action on behalf of our members.

9 The following analysis represents a partial analysis of the material. There is much more that could be done to explore some of the issues at greater depth and areas of major interest, such as the extent of trade union recognition, remain to be completed.

PRELIMINARY FINDINGS FROM THE ANALYSIS

10 Preliminary findings so far suggest that:

The background to going grant-maintained

11   (i) The main reason for seeking grant-maintained status was the fear of closure or reorganisation.

(ii) 25 of the representatives cite the threat of closure or reorganisation as the prime reason for seeking grant-maintained status. Only 7 chose freedom from the LEA.

12 (i) The prime mover in the decision to seek grant-maintained status in comprehensive schools was most likely to be the headteacher.

(ii) 16 representatives make some reference to the role of the headteacher – only 2 selective schools mention the headteacher. In the selective schools 6 chose parents and 6 governors as the prime mover in promoting the proposal – compared to 2 and 5 respectively in the comprehensive schools.

The management of grant-maintained schools

13 (i) Half the schools say there has been no significant change in the management of the school and half those reporting change relate it to the appointment of a bursar and the reallocation of senior management responsibilities. Only 3 make any reference to an increased role in management by the governors. This seems to be unrelated to the date of incorporation.

12 (i) The rise (and likely fall) of the bursar.

(ii) Only 1 school does not report the appointment of a bursar or finance officer. 5 bursars appear to be relatively senior appointments – salaries of £18,000 and £25,000 – of approximately deputy head status and with a role in decision-making. Bureaucratic bursars are already causing irritation.

12 (i) Radical change is rare.

(ii) 1 school mentions appointments such as head of resources and college promotions, advertised at £25,000 per annum, plus a finance officer plus a recently appointed personnel officer. Only 1 refers to a completely new management structure involving teachers.

School planning

16 If we take an emphasis of quality in education as one of the main features of effective schools and one kind of managerial quality that might be expected of the 'flagship' grant-maintained schools, we might expect to see this reflected in a new emphasis on evaluation and monitoring and on planning. Yet when asked 'Has the school discussed the ways of evaluating and monitoring its performance?', to be generous, no more than a third of these schools have given much thought to this.

● 11 selective schools and 17 comprehensive schools' representatives say they have school development plans.

● 5 selective schools and 12 comprehensive schools have staff development plans, although 2 of the selective schools seem not to have made the staff development plans available even to the teaching staff.

Management style

17 As far as teachers in grant-maintained schools are concerned the management style of the school might be seen to be even more important than in a maintained school, even under LMS. It has also been assumed that well managed schools would want to become grant-maintained schools and that grant-maintained schools would be well managed schools. What are the perceptions of AMMA representatives of the current school management and the direction of change, if any, since going grant-maintained?

18 The responses were categorised under 3 headings:

POSITIVE (For example: 'open and friendly'; 'firm, fair, friendly, open and successful!'; 'consultative and approachable').

NEUTRAL (For example: 'ad hockery' (sic); 'means well but inconsistent'; 'a generally benevolent dictatorship').

NEGATIVE (For example: 'authoritarian'; 'autocratic'; 'mysterious').

19 Only 10 out of AMMA's 37 union representatives, whatever their management position, make negative criticisms which seems to suggest that the majority of grant-maintained schools are adequately and appropriately managed.

20 But what, if anything, does this have to do with the grant-maintained status?

Changes in management style

21 Half the selective schools and the vast majority of the comprehensive schools answer yes to the question 'Has there been a noticeable and significant change since becoming a grant-maintained school?' However, approximately one half refer to better physical and financial provision rather than aspects of management itself. It must be said that there are relatively few references to changes that could be specifically related to management style – 3 comprehensive schools mention that it has become more open; and that there is a more positive attitude from headteacher and governors. Equally only 5 chose to refer to a worsening management style. For example, 'less consultation with teachers and an increase in the amount of unnecessary administrative work and a greater tendency to impose management views plus a lack of understanding of the burdens placed on classroom teachers'. There seems to be some indication that grant-maintained status intensifies rather than alters an existing management style.

Teacher morale

22 Perhaps if anything can be related to successful change and positive creative management it is the perception of key staff members that morale is high. It certainly seems to have been an assumption of the government that, with experience, teachers too would appreciate the benefits of greater autonomy. To what extent is this borne out in the perceptions of AMMA's representatives in the 27 schools? Certainly low morale is not unknown. However, over half, 15, of the comprehensive schools are at the very least positive – although 4 of the 7 single sex comprehensive schools report – as do about one third of the selective schools – poor, low or not very good morale. Although the analysis is not yet complete, certainly in the selective schools, the change is likely to be in a negative rather than positive direction. The reverse seems to be the case in comprehensive schools, most particularly co-educational ones, where approximately half report improved morale, largely related to grant-maintained status.

Contracts and conditions of service

23 Representatives were asked whether the school had issued new contracts to existing staff since going grant-maintained and whether there are any significant differences to the 'Burgundy Book' or the conditions of service with the previous LEA. Here there appears to be a significant difference between the selective and comprehensive schools – with only 1 of the former issuing a new contract, compared to 9 of the comprehensive schools. Of these 9, 4 say there is no change to the 'Burgundy Book' or previous conditions. The 2 that mention changes refer to improvements only, for

example, maternity and paternity benefits, sickness arrangements, payment to new teachers – a minimum salary on starting and after three years and sabbatical leave; and a concept of continuous service to include all periods of service in teaching whether here or abroad, public or private. So is, therefore, everything well? More than a quarter of the representatives say these contracts still have to be formulated or are imminent or in progress – at least 1 predicts that 'there could be problems'. On the significant issue of whether all teaching staff enjoy the same contractual conditions whether or not they were appointed after acquiring grant-maintained status, only 4 schools mention any differences. For example, minor changes relating to sickness pay, and one-year contracts paid only to the 31 July, which has created very unhappy feelings and relationships with management.

Directed time

24 The overwhelming majority of grant-maintained schools say that there has been no change to the use of the 1,265 hours directed time.

Directed days

25 There seems to be a significant difference between the answers of selective and comprehensive schools to the question 'Has there been a significant change to the use of the five directed days since going grant-maintained?' Only 1 selective co-educational schools says that the days have been more meaningful compared to 7 of the comprehensive schools which comment, for example, 'Much better training and general use of time'; 'Content better . . . and meet at venues outside the school with excellent facilities and catering'.

Non-contact time

26 Thirteen of the selective schools and 18 of the comprehensive schools report no change to the allocation of non-contact time.

Changes to class size

27 Only 2 of the selective schools and 6 of the comprehensive schools indicate that there has been any change at all to class sizes. There is some indication in half of these of a move towards smaller classes or plans to do so in the future. The most dramatic is confined to a single school which has reduced junior classes from 33 to 28 and to a maximum of 30, often 20, in option groups resulting in an increase of staffing of 6. Equally there is some indication of an increase in class size possibly due to the effect of grant-maintained status itself.

Use of support staff

28 Two of the selective schools, but 10 of the comprehensive schools report a significant increase in the use of support staff. However, the references are overwhelming to administrative staff. Two schools mention more supply cover. Only one other comment seems to relate positively to the educational life of the school in that there is more organisation now that there is a head of learning support.

Teaching groups and teaching activities

29 Very few schools report any change in teaching groups or in teaching activities. Only 6–2 selective and 4 comprehensive – mention this at all. One of the latter has reintroduced setting instead of banding. The most significant, and an exceptional example, is the employment of two extra special-needs teachers allowing pupils to be withdrawn from lessons for testing and diagnosing their learning problems and work on a one-to-one basis, plus another two special-needs teachers available to provide support in subject areas.

Physical provision and facilities for students and staff

30 At least one might have expected that grant-maintained schools would have used some of their generous capital allocations to benefit the staff of the school.

31 Amongst the selective schools only 1 is prepared to say that things have already improved and that only marginally. Most of the improved carpeting, furniture, refurbishment and accommodation is planned or promised. Things have advanced much further in the comprehensive schools. Almost all report improvements. Programmes of redecoration, re-carpeting and refurnishing are widespread – as one school states 'every aspect has got significantly better'.

32 In contrast, over half – 8 – of the selective schools report improvement for students. Four refer to catering facilities, another 3 schools refer to improvements to the sixth form – as one representative, perhaps perceptively, says 'this could be related to the numbers game'.

33 The comprehensive schools show a similar emphasis on providing or refurbishing, especially re-carpeting, sixth-form common rooms, although, unlike the selective schools, fewer of these schools had improved provision for students than had done so for staff. Refitting, refurbishing and carpeting were much mentioned. Two grander projects were technology and music areas refurbished at great expense and urgently needed building repairs completed, new stage and lighting systems plus stage curtains and hall curtains, an old and poorly equipped home economics room converted into a restaurant area for pupils on catering courses to use, a new ventilation system for the craft area, and a classroom converted into a multi-gym for pupils – perhaps unbelievably all the last five in the same school. To the less fortunate it may be some consolation to know that 1 school reports plans turned down by the DES.

Facilities

34 Over half the schools claimed to have extended the provision of copying facilities, secretarial support for senior management and for teachers, and fax machines as a consequence of going grant-maintained. The most striking difference between the selective and the comprehensive schools were that 10 of the comprehensive schools had provided secretarial support for the staff compared to 2 of the selective schools – although 1 was planning to do so – the figures for secretarial support for senior management were 14 and 8 respectively, 3 of the schools claimed to have added the complete list of copying facilities, desk-top publishing, secretarial support for senior management and teachers, ancillary staff, technical support staff, fax facilities, information technology and online databases.

Staffing

35 When asked whether staffing has increased, decreased or stayed the same, only 2 selective schools mention a decrease but this is not attributable, in their view, to grant-maintained status – 7 of the selective schools and 10 of the comprehensive schools say that staffing has stayed the same. Of the remainder many quite properly point out that the increase is due to increased numbers and by that interpretation the staffing has not increased. A clear intention to increase the overall staffing can be seen in only 4 schools, 1 selective school expects to increase the staff by 6 by September 1991, because of its decisions to reduce junior class sizes and to increase technical provision. Where figures are quoted, that of 6 is quite exceptional – the range is between 1 and 2.8.

Non-teaching staff

36 Over half the schools report an increase.

Change in employment practice

37 AMMA was interested to examine whether there had been an increase in part-time appointments, temporary appointments and fixed-term contracts. Any detrimental changes appear to be limited, but it is of concern that 1 school has more contracts on a one-year probationary basis and another issues contracts varying from 1 to 5 years in length, although all teachers at the schools 'still have their indefinite contracts – as far as I know'.

Premature retirement and the special purpose grant

38 All but 3 of the representatives in selective schools quoted examples of early retirement compared to only 6 of the comprehensive schools. There are examples of its extensive use, for example, in the selective schools – 1 school reports 5 staff leaving, three each 4. Nor is this unknown in comprehensive schools. One school reports, details not fully public, but five premature retirements in the course of 6 months. In general, though it appears that the selective schools have made much greater use overall of the special purposes grant and premature retirements. This may account for the fact that, whereas 4 of the selective schools thought that the staff might not have been content with the arrangements, none of the comprehensive schools suggested this.

Retirement before the change of status

39 However, the position is quite the opposite when representatives responded to the question of whether teachers took premature retirement before going grant-maintained, because of the change of status. There were 5 reports of retirements related wholly or partly to this – two referring to staff, including very senior staff, clearly and explicitly disagreeing with grant-maintained status – all in co-educational schools.

Redundancy

40 Only 1 of the schools mentions redundancy, other than premature retirement, for any teacher and this appears to have been mutually convenient.

Salaries

41 It is likely that one of the most difficult areas upon which to find information is that of salaries, particularly the discretionary salary increases paid to senior staff under the new pay flexibilities.

42 Of the 14 selective schools 3 reported movement up the pay scale for headteachers and deputy headteachers, but 4 admit to knowing nothing about this aspect of senior management salaries – only 1 of the schools mentioned any additional payments to staff – an annual bonus of £100.

43 In the 23 comprehensive schools 8 report movement up the pay scale for headteachers and 7 for deputy headteachers. Three of the same schools have paid an annual bonus to all staff and 1 has paid all staff a salary increase. Of the 3 that have paid the annual bonus 2 have also given all staff a salary increase. Of the 8 schools paying the headteacher an increase only 4 do not report some form of increase for all or some staff. One school which reports increases for deputy headteachers and headteacher also reports increases for senior management but nothing for other teachers. One school reports increases for senior management only. Schools reporting 'don't know' on senior management questions do not, apart from one example, indicate overall increases for all staff.

Extension of the standard scale

44 Very few schools report the use of the extension to the salary scale. Only one of the selective schools refers to help for certain colleagues with incremental progression, incentives and local allowances. In the comprehensive schools there seems more use of this on a temporary and discretionary basis.

Incentive allowances

45 Six of the 14 selective schools and 10 of the 23 comprehensive schools report a more extensive use of incentive allowances, although of the former one denies that this is related to GMS. In practice, the use of allowances seems to be little more than a 'few extra A allowances' for minor responsibilities and specific teaching responsibilities. Only 2 representatives report more use of B allowances, and in one of them C allowances, but for the former there is some suggestion in a previous response that these may be temporary allowances. One school reports fifteen members of staff receiving allowances or increased allowances from next September with several having receiving allowances last September. This is in a school which does not report any salary increases to senior management. Of those that say 'yes' to this question, 6 do not report any known salary increase for senior management.

Tentative conclusions and possible further lines of investigation

46 Financial autonomy alone – even with additional money – may be insufficient to raise morale and change or enhance a school's sense of direction and

purposefulness. It is highly relevant to LMS if any schools that have positively chosen this route via grant-maintained status report declining morale.

47 Seeking grant-maintained status as a defensive protective route – as for the selective schools and, to some extent, the single-sex comprehensive schools – may not be the way to unlock its possible potential.

48 The leadership of headteachers, as opposed to the will of parents and governors, may be much more significant than the government has appreciated in maximising the flexibility given by financial autonomy and additional resources, and in working towards school improvements as seen in increased morale.

49 The leadership and management styles of the comprehensive co-educational schools which have opted out might bear more intensive examination if we are to learn anything about adaptable and creative management.

50 Money does help. Teachers are affected by improvements to the physical conditions and to the school and its facilities.

51 There may be a 'Hawthorne' effect in the schools that have been the first to go grant-maintained. Feeling special and different, feeling favoured or even that you are going 'against the odds' may have raised morale and purposiveness. If grant-maintained status were commonplace and the available money reduced, would it be any impetus to improvement and raised morale?

52 LEA bureaucracy and inefficiency is not the only form of bureaucracy and inefficiency. The polarisation of the administration and educational aims of a school is a genuine irritation to teachers as is school bureaucracy and financial mismanagement.

53 Where there is LEA hostility and hostility from former professional colleagues some teachers feel this acutely. Forced isolation could be the result in many grant-maintained schools. It could have an effect on the type of recruitment to grant-maintained schools in certain areas in the longer term. As yet there is no evidence of teachers in grant-maintained schools choosing to replace this with intra-sector support.

54 The direct predictions of radically altered employment practice are not borne out – as yet. For teachers' unions the casework implications are more likely to arise because a school is badly managed than because it is GMS rather than LMS.

55 Educational improvements have not been an early priority – the few dramatic modifications suggest that they could have been.

56 There is some suggestion that going grant-maintained polarises and intensifies an existing management style. Will/does LMS do the same?

57 There is some evidence that grant-maintained status empowers both teachers and teacher governors.

58 The use of money (for example, should there be student facilities or staff facilities? – managerial salary incentives or across the board payments? – money spent on salaries or on changes to conditions in the physical environment?) and its effect on morale, is worth further investigation.

59 Very few of the representatives are indifferent to the experience of going grant-maintained. Teachers have no status in the decision to go grant-maintained yet, as employees, they are most closely affected. Their considered views of the experience, its benefits and disadvantages, now deserve a more considered analysis before the models of financial autonomy or individual school autonomy are assumed to be the key factors in change and improvement.

Index